VOLCANOES

Geology is largely history, but volcanoes are as current as life and death. Spirit Lake, formed during eruptions of Mount St. Helens about 1000 B.C., was alive with spring on May 12, 1980, and undisturbed by small new eruptions from the volcano's summit (*previous page*). On May 18, 1980, a giant explosive eruption and avalanche destroyed the entire region surrounding the lake in moments (*above*). Not a tree is left standing; everywhere is barrenness. But Earth abides; life will return to Spirit Lake over the centuries as it did before. (Photographs by the U.S. Geological Survey.)

VOLCANOES

Robert Decker and Barbara Decker
DARTMOUTH COLLEGE

W. H. FREEMAN AND COMPANY
New York

A Series of Books in Geology
Editor: Allan Cox

Project Editor: Judith Wilson
Copy Editor: Ruth Veres
Designer: Robert Ishi
Production Coordinator: William Murdock
Illustration Coordinators: Cheryl Nufer and Audre Loverde
Artist: John Waller
Compositor: York Graphic Services, Inc.
Printer and Binder: The Maple-Vail Book Manufacturing Group

Library of Congress Cataloging in Publication Data
Decker, Robert Wayne, 1927—
 Volcanoes.

 (A Series of books in geology)
 Bibliography: p.
 Includes index.
 1. Volcanoes. I. Decker, Barbara, 1929— joint
author. II. Title.
QE521.D32   551.2′1   80-20126
ISBN 0-7167-1241-5
ISBN 0-7167-1242-3 (pbk.)

Printed in the United States of America

5 6 7 8 9 VB 5 4 3 2 1 0 8 9 8 7

Contents

Preface   vii
Active Volcanoes of the World   viii

1 **Seams of the Earth**   1
2 **Surtsey, Iceland**   15
3 **Fire under the Sea**   29
4 **Krakatau, West of Java**   43
5 **Ring of Fire**   57
6 **Kilauea, Hawaii**   69
7 **Hot Spots**   87
8 **Lava, Ash, and Bombs**   101
9 **Cones and Craters**   117
10 **Roots of Volcanoes**   133
11 **Origin of the Sea and Air**   145
12 **Volcanic Power**   153
13 **Volcanic Treasures**   167
14 **Volcanoes and Climate**   177
15 **Forecasting Volcanic Eruptions**   187

Glossary   209
Appendix A   The World's 101 Most Notorious Volcanoes   215
Appendix B   Volcano Information Centers of the World   231
Appendix C   Metric–English Conversion Table   234
Bibliography   237
Index   241

Preface

Volcanoes assail the senses. They are beautiful in repose and awesome in eruption; they hiss and roar, they smell of brimstone. Their heat warms, their fires consume; they are the homes of Gods and Goddesses.

Volcanoes are described in words and pictures, but they must be experienced to be known. Their roots reach deep inside the Earth, their products are scattered in the sky. Understanding volcanoes is an unconquered challenge. This book poses more questions than answers; such is the harvest of curiosity.

Any book about volcanoes is bound to be highly descriptive, but we have tried to look behind these spectacular phenomena and to emphasize the processes involved. Our book is written for anyone—from student to expert—who is interested in learning more about how volcanoes work.

The style of our text is informal. Specific references are made only in the illustrations. The Bibliography reflects only part of our debt to the hundreds of students of volcanoes whose general knowledge of volcanic processes and products we have used. Dr. James Moore of the U.S. Geological Survey deserves special acknowledgment. We have studied and written about volcanoes together for many years, and it is difficult to say where his thoughts stop and our words begin. We are also grateful to Dr. Allan Cox for the help and advice he has given us in preparing the manuscript.

June 1980   *Robert Decker*
                                                  Barbara Decker

Active Volcanoes of the World

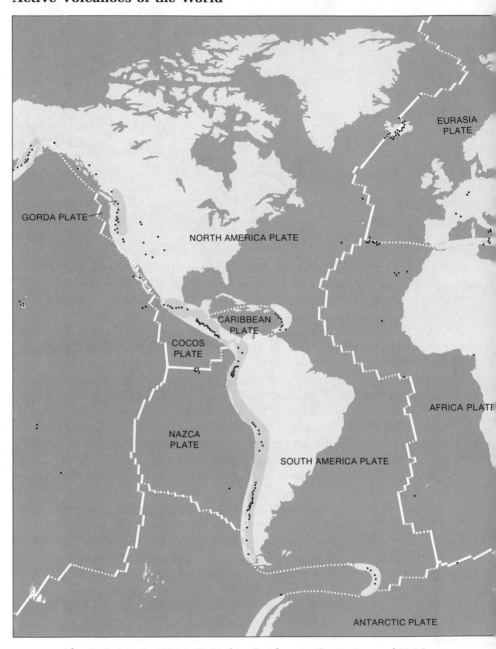

After L. D. Morris, NOAA; T. Simkin, Smithsonian Institution; and H. Meyers, NOAA.

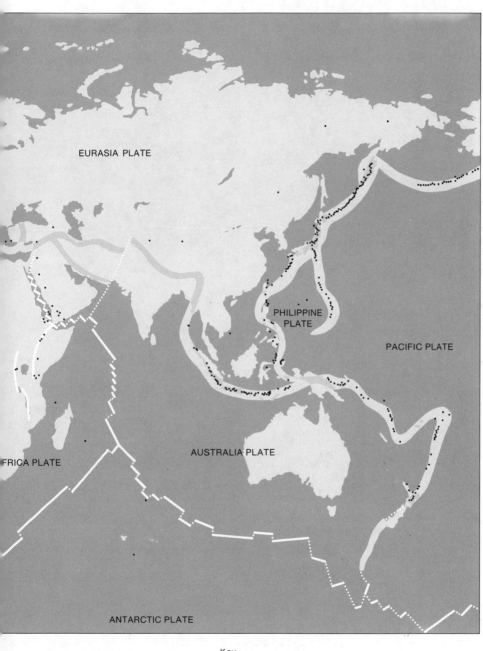

EURASIA PLATE

PHILIPPINE
PLATE

PACIFIC PLATE

FRICA PLATE

AUSTRALIA PLATE

ANTARCTIC PLATE

Key

Rift zones

Strike-slip (transform) faults

Subduction zones

• Geologically young volcanoes

VOLCANOES

1
Seams of the Earth

1 Seams of the Earth

Nature knows no pause in progress and development,
and attaches her curse to all inaction.
Goethe (1749–1832)

The matching shores of eastern South America and western Africa form an intriguing jigsaw puzzle. Did Brazil's bulge once fit against the Congo? Did some great supercontinent break up and drift apart, each piece forming one of our present continents?

Alfred Wegener, an Austrian scientist, championed the concept of continental drift for twenty years until his death on the Greenland Icecap in 1930. He noted not only that the edges of the continents make a rough fit, but also that the Appalachian mountain range in eastern North America breaks off abruptly in Newfoundland and reappears across the Atlantic Ocean in Ireland, Scotland, and Scandinavia. He argued that the similarity of European and American fossils until 180 million years ago and the dissimilarity of more recent fossils is one more piece of evidence that the continents as we know them are still-drifting segments of an ancient supercontinent.

Wegener also recognized that the Earth's surface has two predominant elevations: one between sea level and 1000 meters above sea level, the other between 4000 and 5000 meters below sea level (Figure 1). He hypothesized that this difference in elevation between continents and oceans was caused by differences in the density and thickness of rocks in the continental blocks compared to oceanic crust. He believed that the lighter and thicker continental blocks floated above the oceanic crust like icebergs drifting through the sea.

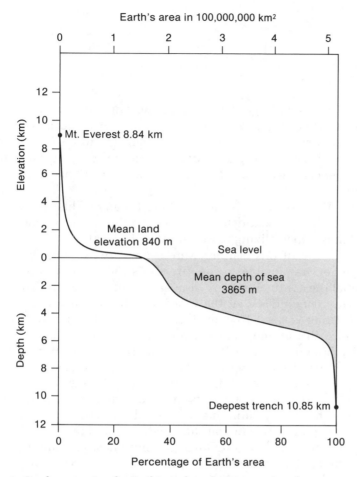

Earth's area in 100,000,000 km²

1 Graph comparing the Earth's surface elevations and surface areas. The two benches on the curve reflect the basically different thicknesses and densities of continental and oceanic crust. (Adapted from Alyn C. Duxbury, *The Earth and Its Oceans*. © 1971 Addison-Wesley, Reading, Massachusetts. Fig. 3.2, Reprinted with permission.)

To understand his use of "float" and "drift," one must understand the geologist's concept of crust and time. Wegener envisioned the oceanic crust as being more viscous than tar or pitch, so that the "floating" took thousands of years to reach balance, and the "drifting" proceeded even more slowly.

Continental drift was one of the great scientific controversies of its day, and Wegener's arguments in favor of it were alluring. Wegener called the great supercontinent he envisioned Pangaea: it was so large that it contained both the polar scars of ancient ice ages and the equatorial legacy of vast coal swamps which existed before its breakup. According to his theory, the present locations of glacial deposits near the equator and the coal deposits near the current poles are the result of continental drift.

But Wegener was also a zealot, and many of his contemporaries, wary of too much zeal, considered him a crackpot. Geophysicists specializing in the study of the Earth's interior in the first quarter of this century were especially skeptical because Wegener was unable to identify the strong forces needed to propel the continents away from each other. These experts had already concluded that the interior of the Earth was as solid and strong as steel. To them, the notion that floating continents could drift through such a strong "sea" seemed untenable.

Their knowledge of the deep interior of the Earth came mainly from analyzing what happens to earthquake waves as they propagate through the Earth. This approach to Earth science is called seismology. Its methods are similar to the doctor's technique of thumping on your chest to discover whether there is liquid or air in your lungs: differences in the quality of the thump sound passing through your chest provide the key. Seismology is a rigorous discipline based on precise physical principles and its conclusions are well respected by all geologists. The denial of continental drift on such geophysical objections was convincing despite the good circumstantial evidence in its favor, and the hypothesis went underground for thirty years.

However, among geologists there is a half-joke called Smith's Law which states that anything that did happen, can happen. So even without understanding how the large horizontal movement of continents could happen, some geologists still looked for evidence that it did happen.

The breakthrough that proved Wegener was right came in 1960 from marine geophysicists analyzing the Earth's magnetic field over the ocean floor. They found that the magnetic field was unusually strong directly over the oceanic ridges. The reason, they proposed, is that the rocks making up the ridge contain iron-rich minerals and are magnetized parallel to the Earth's magnetic field, which tends to reinforce that field.

As the geophysicists extended their surveys away from the ridges, they found that the magnetic field at the surface of the sea was a zebra-striped pattern of alternating belts of unusually high and unusually low intensity. Their explanation of the low-intensity belts was that the ocean floor beneath them had formed at times when the Earth's magnetic field pointed to the *south*, rather than to the north as it does today.

By the time of the marine magnetic surveys in 1960, geophysicists studying the magnetic properties and ages of lavas on land had already demonstrated that the Earth's magnetic field periodically switches from north to south and back again. The time between reversals may be as short as 30,000 years or as long as several million years. Using this magnetic reversal time scale, the marine geophysicists knew when the field had flipped, and they could estimate the age of the ocean floor beneath each magnetic stripe. The stage was set for a dramatic new idea.

Geologists now proposed that instead of continents drifting *through* the ocean floor, the seafloor spread away from the oceanic ridges as it formed, carrying the continents along as part of large, spreading plates (Figure 2). The new idea was called seafloor spreading or *plate tectonics*, and the magnetic stripes gave a record of both the geometry and the rate of spreading, or plate movements. The pattern and ages of the magnetic stripes parallel to the ocean's ridge systems provide a giant slow-motion tape recording of the Earth's horizontal movements over the past 100 million years.

The pattern that has emerged shows the Earth's surface broken into about 10 plates which are moving in various directions relative to one another. The margins or seams between the plates are of three basic types: *compressional*, where the plates override one another; *extensional*, where the plates break apart; and side-slipping or *strike-slip,* where the plates slide by one another without separating or overriding (Figures 3 and 4).

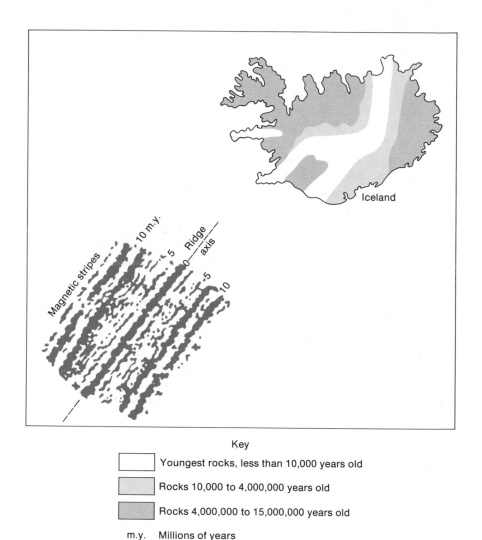

Key

Youngest rocks, less than 10,000 years old

Rocks 10,000 to 4,000,000 years old

Rocks 4,000,000 to 15,000,000 years old

m.y.   Millions of years

2 Magnetic field strength measured at the sea surface southwest of Iceland shows a definite striped pattern parallel to the axis of the Mid-Atlantic ridge. The symmetry of the pattern on either side of the ridge and the similar pattern in the ages of volcanic rocks in Iceland are strong evidence that the seafloor spreads away from the ridge axis. (After Charles Drake, "The Geological Revolution," Condon Lectures, Oregon State System of Higher Education, Eugene, Oregon, 1970.)

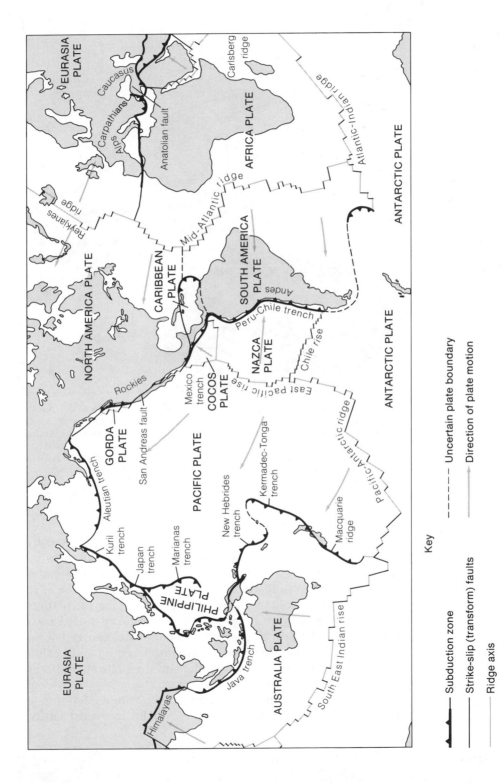

3 Rigid plates of the Earth's surface are slowly moving horizontally away from and toward one another. The arrows shown assume that the Africa plate is not moving. Plates separate along the crests of mid-ocean ridges, slide past each other along strike-slip faults, and converge at subduction zones. (After J. F. Dewey, "Plate Tectonics." Copyright © 1972 by Scientific American, Inc. All rights reserved.)

Key

━━━ Subduction zone
──── Strike-slip (transform) faults
──── Ridge axis
----- Uncertain plate boundary
──→ Direction of plate motion

EURASIA PLATE
⤋ EURASIA PLATE
Caucasus
Carpathians
Alps
Anatolian fault
Carlsberg ridge
AFRICA PLATE
Reykjanes ridge
Mid-Atlantic ridge
Atlantic-Indian ridge
ANTARCTIC PLATE
NORTH AMERICA PLATE
CARIBBEAN PLATE
SOUTH AMERICA PLATE
Andes
Peru-Chile trench
Chile rise
NAZCA PLATE
East Pacific rise
COCOS PLATE
Mexico trench
Rockies
San Andreas fault
GORDA PLATE
Aleutian trench
Kuril trench
Japan trench
Marianas trench
PACIFIC PLATE
New Hebrides trench
Kermadec-Tonga trench
Macquarie ridge
Pacific-Antarctic ridge
ANTARCTIC PLATE
PHILIPPINE PLATE
Java trench
Himalayas
AUSTRALIA PLATE
South East Indian rise
EURASIA PLATE

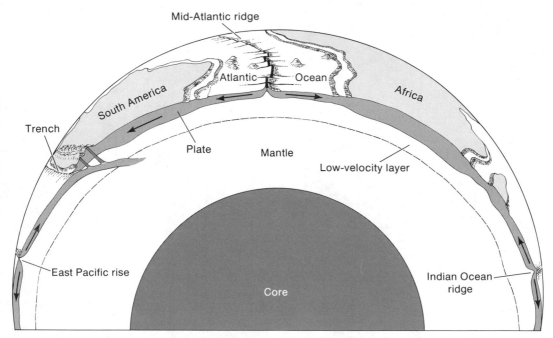

4 Movement of plates shown in a cross section of the Earth. The Africa and South America plates separate along the Mid-Atlantic ridge at a rate of a few inches per year. The South America and Nazca (East Pacific Ocean) plates converge to form the Andes Mountains. The thickness of the plates and the low-velocity layer on which they move is exaggerated so that they can be shown at this small scale. (After K.C. Burke and J. Tuzo Wilson, "Hot Spots on the Earth's Surface." Copyright © 1976 by Scientific American, Inc. All rights reserved.)

Compressional and extensional margins are characterized by different types of volcanic activity and strike-slip margins by almost no volcanism, so the link between plate tectonics and volcanism is close indeed.

Earthquakes, topography, and other geological structures identify the three types of seams. At the compressional margins, also known as *subduction zones,* one plate, generally oceanic, pushes beneath the other. This causes earthquakes originating near the surface seam or in the sinking plate at depths as great as 700 kilometers. Physical forces at the compressional margin cause the ocean floor to bend down into a deep trench while the edge of the upper plate is broken by thrust faults.

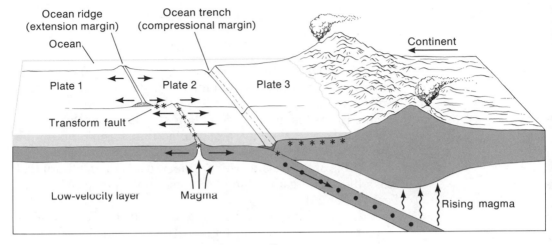

Ocean ridge
(extension margin)

Ocean trench
(compressional margin)

Continent

Ocean

Plate 1   Plate 2   Plate 3

Transform fault

Low-velocity layer   Magma   Rising magma

Key

* Shallow earthquakes
(tension on ridges; lateral slip on transform faults)

• Deep earthquakes
(mainly showing thrusting and down-dip compression)

5 Schematic cross section of plate margins showing the association of earthquakes with the plate boundaries formed by ocean ridges, strike-slip (transform) faults, and subduction zones. (After L. Sykes et al., in F. Press and R. Siever, *Earth*, First Edition, p. 644. W.H. Freeman and Company, Copyright ©, 1974.)

Rock layers scraped off the ocean floor are squeezed into accordion folds against the upper plate. The geological result is an island arc like Japan or a mountain chain like the Andes.

At extensional margins, the earthquakes are shallow and follow the center of the rift. The center of the rift is often a valley formed by the separating plates (Figure 5). No folds are formed because the area is being stretched, not squeezed, and the fractures are either open cracks or slumps called normal faults. Most extensional margins are submarine, and new oceanic crust is formed at the separating edges; the crust grows outward from the oceanic ridges near the centers of the world's major oceans. The main ridges are the Mid-Atlantic ridge, the East Pacific ridge, and the Central Indian Ocean ridge. They are broad, rugged, submarine mountain ranges a few kilometers high, a few thousand kilometers wide, and tens of thousands of kilometers long. Drain away the oceans and you would be able to see the greatest mountain system on Earth.

The strike-slip plate margins (called *transform faults* in the jargon of plate tectonics) are also mainly submarine. They connect offsets of the oceanic ridges into a rectangular pattern that looks like an alligator's hide on topographical maps of the sea floor (Figure 6).

Sometimes a slice of continent gets involved in the shearing of a side-slipping margin; the San Andreas fault in California is the classic example of a transform fault on land. Los Angeles is moving northwest relative to San Francisco at a rate of about 5 centimeters per year. However, society will probably make them one city well before nature slides the two together. Shallow earthquakes, linear valleys, and twisted rocks mark the strike-slip plate margins (Figure 7).

Despite the overwhelming evidence that seafloor spreading takes place, the strength and solidity of the Earth's interior remained a problem that seismologists have only recently resolved. This is ironic since it was the seismologists whose arguments had shot down Wegener's hypothesis in the 1920s. Looking closely at earthquake wave records, particularly those from underground nuclear bomb tests with precisely known locations and times of origin, they discovered a zone about 100 to 200 kilometers beneath the Earth's surface where seismic waves travel unusually slowly and are partially absorbed.

6 Topographical map of the Atlantic Ocean with the water drained away. The Mid-Atlantic Ridge is one of the world's greatest mountain ranges. The breaks perpendicular to the valley crest of the ridge are called fracture zones or transform faults—other terms for strike-slip margins. (From *World Ocean Floor Panorama* by Bruce C. Heezen and Marie Tharp, initiated and supported by the Office of Naval Research. Copyright Marie Tharp, 1977. Reproduced by permission of Marie Tharp, all rights reserved.)

7 San Andreas fault cutting across the Elkhorn and Carrizo Plains in south-central California. The North America plate is on the right and the Pacific plate is on the left. Movement on the fault is right lateral, so called because for a person standing on either plate, the sense of motion on the opposite plate is to the right. (Photograph by Robert E. Wallace, U.S. Geological Survey.)

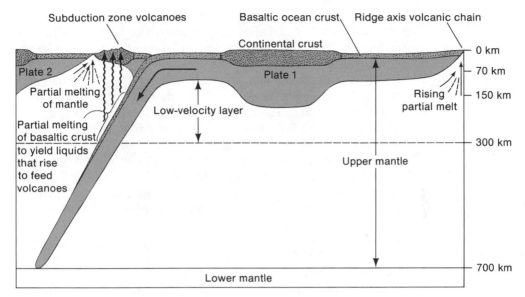

8 Cross section of the Earth's upper mantle. The rigid plate is composed of solidified rock that moves on the partially molten low-velocity layer. The plates are approximately 70 kilometers thick under oceans and 100 to 150 kilometers thick under continents. The continents are parts of the plates and move with them. (After J.F. Dewey, "Plate Tectonics." Copyright © 1972 by Scientific American. All rights reserved.)

This low-velocity layer is not very strong; it probably contains a small percentage of molten rock. The characteristics of this layer provide a reasonable explanation for plate motions and for the deep source of volcanoes. The plates slide on the soft, low-velocity layer under the influence of very small horizontal forces, and fractures in the Earth's crust at the extensional plate margins allow the partially molten rock to leak to the surface, forming volcanoes (Figure 8).

Wegener turned out to be a prophet, although his original idea has been significantly changed. He believed the continents drifted like isolated rafts through a viscous oceanic crust. The theory of seafloor spreading envisions rigid plates of oceanic crust forming and spreading from the ocean ridges; the continental blocks are carried like rafts frozen into the larger plates, which are composed of both oceanic and continental crust.

In the last two decades of unprecedented progress in our understanding of the Earth, the development and rapid acceptance of the concept of seafloor spreading stands as one of the grand moments in science. Not only can the jigsaw puzzle of the continents be reconstructed, but their ongoing movements can be determined. The dynamics of plate motions control both earthquakes and volcanoes, which occur for the most part on the creaking and leaking margins of the plates.

The association between volcanoes and earthquake belts has long been recognized. Aristotle proposed that earthquakes were caused by the rumbling of pent-up gases which were eventually vented at volcanoes; he recognized the connection even though we wouldn't agree with his explanation today. Perhaps the most important lesson of the past two decades has been the virtue of scientific humility; who knows which ideas that now appear untenable will turn out to be right, and which of those ideas that we currently accept on the basis of available evidence will seem hopelessly naive two thousand years from now?

2
Surtsey, Iceland

2 Surtsey, Iceland

*At three o'clock in the morning we saw smoke rising
from the sea and thought it to be land; but on closer
consideration we concluded that this was a special
wonder wrought by God and that a natural sea could burn.*
Captain Jorgen Mindelberg
Iceland (1783)

Iceland sits astride the Mid-Atlantic ridge, part of the world-wide rift system. This 300-by-500-kilometer island whose north shore touches the Arctic Circle is entirely volcanic in origin. Eruptions occur about every five years; sometimes from distinct volcanoes like Mount Hekla, which has erupted 15 times since 1000 A.D., but often from long fissures that erupt only once. Iceland grows in size from volcanic eruptions, and is worn away by the storms of the North Atlantic. Icelandic farmers and fishermen know the Earth is a dynamic place; they are all geologists at heart.

The story of the Surtsey eruption begins at sea. Icelandic volcanologist Sigurdur Thorarinsson has been its chronicler.

At 7:15 AM on November 14, 1963, Olafur Vestmann, the cook on a fishing boat off the south coast of Iceland, noticed dark smoke on the horizon against the half-light of dawn. Since no land existed in that direction the first alarm was that a ship was on fire, but soon the fishermen recognized that the black columns of volcanic ash signaled an eruption from beneath the sea. By 11 AM the eruption cloud of ash and steam had reached a height of 3500 meters, and volcanologists were on their way to observe the eruption from the air.

At 11:30 AM the eruption was coming from three submarine vents along a northeast–southwest line. Explosions from the vents were occurring every few seconds, shooting jets of dense black ash to heights of 100 to 150 meters. By 3 PM the separate

9 Column of steam and ash rising over 3000 meters from the Surtsey eruption on November 16, 1963, two days after the eruption was first sighted. (Photograph by Hjálmar Bárdarson.)

eruption columns had joined along a 500-meter line across the sea surface, and the rapid emission of black volcanic debris indicated that a new island was about to form. Surtsey, named for Surtur, the mythological giant of fire, was born that night (Figure 9).

The eruption was a surprise. Only in hindsight were the few clues to a forthcoming eruption recognized. Two days before the eruption, a marine research vessel had noticed a strange

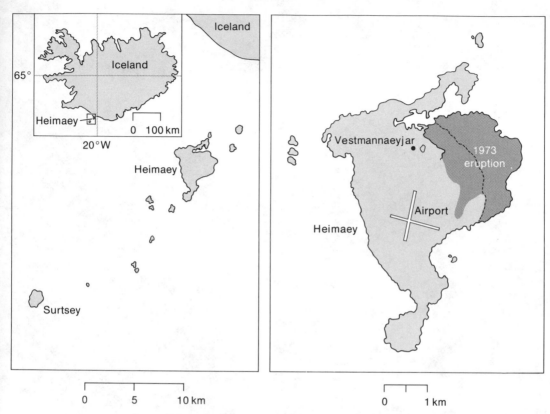

10 Map of the Vestmann Islands showing Surtsey, which formed in 1963–1967, and Heimaey, which formed in prehistoric times. The shaded area represents lava added to Heimaey during the 1973 eruption. The former shore is shown by a dotted line.

rise in the temperature of the sea surface above the normal 7°C to 9°C in an area about 3 kilometers from the eruption site. Also on November 12, people in Vik, a coastal village 80 kilometers east of Surtsey, had noticed the rotten-egg smell of hydrogen sulfide (H_2S). The seismograph at Reykjavik, 120 kilometers away, had recorded weak tremors a week before the eruption was first observed, but the location of the seismic disturbance could not be determined. No preliminary earthquakes were felt at the fishing port of Vestmannaeyjar on Heimaey Island 22 kilometers northeast of Surtsey, the closest settlement to the eruption (Figure 10).

Presumably the eruption began quietly at 130 meters below sea level and took days or weeks to build the volcano to just beneath the sea surface. There, the explosive activity could no longer be contained and quenched by the pressure and chill of the sea.

During the first week, the new island erupted and grew almost continuously. Closely spaced explosions merging into a steady jetting of volcanic ash formed a towering column that rose to a height of 9 kilometers.

By November 18, Surtsey was a ridge 550 meters long and 45 meters high, split lengthwise by the erupting fissure. Gradually one vent along the fissure became dominant and the island began to grow more circular. On November 24 the island was 900 meters long, 650 meters wide, and the rim of the main crater was almost 100 meters high. The entire island was built of loose dark volcanic debris, thrown out in fragments by the explosive eruptions. Lava flows of liquid rock had not yet begun, and the loose volcanic pile was an easy target for the strong winter storms of the North Atlantic. However, the eruption more than kept pace with marine erosion and slumping. By February 5, 1964, the maximum height of the volcanic island was 174 meters and the maximum diameter 1300 meters, including a wave-cut terrace around the shore with a width of about 150 meters.

During the first three months of the eruption, the sea had easy access to the erupting vents, both by direct flooding and by seepage through the loose volcanic pile. This contact with water produced the steam explosions which characterize shallow submarine eruptions. Each explosion expelled a black mass of rock fragments, out of which shot numerous larger fragments of pasty lava called volcanic bombs. The bombs left trails of black volcanic ash which rapidly turned white and furry as the hot, invisible steam in the trails cooled and condensed. The black jetlike arcs turning greyish white gave the

11 Black jets of ash explode to heights of 250 meters during the Surtsey eruption. Jet trails follow behind large volcanic bombs that whistle as they spin in flight. (Photograph by Thorleifur Einarsson.)

eruptions the appearance of an exploding fireworks factory (Figure 11). The bombs whistled as they spun in flight, and often landed in the sea more than a kilometer from the vent. The steam explosions themselves were peculiarly quiet, beginning with a muted thump and an almost silent burst of debris.

When the explosions occurred in rapid sequence, as they often did, a large ash and steam cloud rose above the island. On the rare calm days this plume reached as high as 10 kilometers, but generally the strong winds bent the column at 500 to 2000 meters and caused ash falls many kilometers downwind, some of which contaminated the water supply caught on the roofs in Vestmannaeyjar. The violent updrafts of air into the ash cloud

12 Lightning bolts discharge the buildup of electricity in the uprushing ash column at Surtsey. Ninety-second time-exposure. (Photograph by Sigurgeir Jónasson, December 1, 1963.)

caused whirlwinds, waterspouts, lightning flashes, and some-times hailstones of falling volcanic fragments coated with ice (Figure 12).

At times the explosive eruptions changed into a continuous uprush of volcanic fragments and steam. Bombs, glowing red to orange, lit the uprushing column at night. Only brief lulls in the eruption occurred during November and December, but by January there were periods of repose lasting up to a day. As the island grew, seawater was more effectively blocked from the crater and the steam explosions diminished.

In April, fire fountains and lava flows became the dominant activity, forming a capping of hard, solid rocks over the lower

13 During 1964 Surtsey grew until the sea was blocked from the vent area. As a result, the eruption changed from explosions to incandescent lava fountains and flows. White steam clouds arising where the flows entered the sea replaced the black and gray explosion clouds. (Photograph by Captain Gardar Pálsson.)

slopes of Surtsey (Figure 13). The island was now assured a place on the maps of the world; the waves still pounded on the shores but they met their match on the hardened lavas. The quiet effusion of lava continued for more than a year as Surtsey increased in area to 2.5 square kilometers, more than half capped by hard lava flows (Figure 14).

During 1965 and 1966, small explosive eruptions built low islands of volcanic debris both northeast and southwest of Surtsey, but these loose volcanic piles were not large or armored with lava flows and were soon washed away by oceanic storms.

In August 1966 renewed lava eruptions issued from the main crater on Surtsey. The lava flowed continuously in tunnels beneath its own crust to the edges of the island. We visited Surtsey during this last activity and were amazed to see that the orange tongues of lava pouring from the tunnels into the sea still glowed as they plunged beneath the waves. The insulating effects of the chilled skin and the steam layer on the surface of the lava were so effective that they prevented rapid quenching and steam explosions.

By June 1967 the eruption was over; it had lasted $3^1/_2$ years. The total volume of volcanic ash and lava was slightly more than 1 cubic kilometer; only 9 percent of that was above sea level. The rates of eruption were highest in the early phases and diminished more or less continuously during the course of the activity. The lava temperatures on emission averaged about 1140°C.

The eruption had three main phases. First, there was the quiet, undetected underwater buildup from 130 meters below sea level to a few meters below sea level, possibly lasting several weeks. Second, explosive eruptions from shallow water built an island of loose volcanic debris. This was the beginning of the observable eruption. Third, the blocking of water from the vent stopped the explosions and allowed the quiet emission of lava flows (Figure 15).

The shape of Surtsey reflects the island's three-part volcanic history. The underwater base is steep-sided from the rapid cooling and piling up of the submarine lavas; the explosive debris forms steep crater walls and cones above sea level but has been cut into a flat bench at sea level by wave erosion; the final lava flows form gentle slopes where they poured out and hardened over the loose debris from earlier explosions.

Surtsey was born in sea, steam, and fire. Its rock ribs were molded by the environment into which it erupted. The Earth is shaped by such conflicting forces over immense spans of time. It is rare to witness these events condensed into just four years.

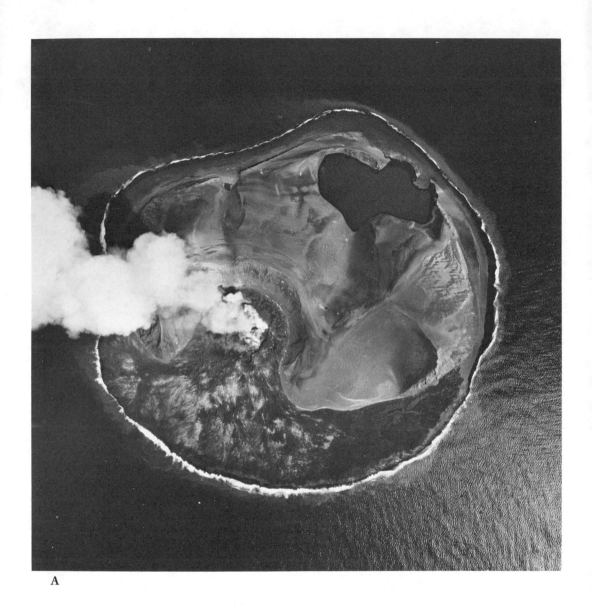

A

14 Aerial photographs looking down vertically on the growing Island of Surtsey (about 1.3 kilometers in diameter when photographed). The light gray area is covered by volcanic ash and cinders. The dark areas in the south are basaltic lava flows extending into the sea, which cover the loose explosive debris and protect it from erosion by the waves. The dark area in the north is a lagoon. A. June 18, 1964. B. August 25, 1964. (Photographs by Landmaelingar Islands.)

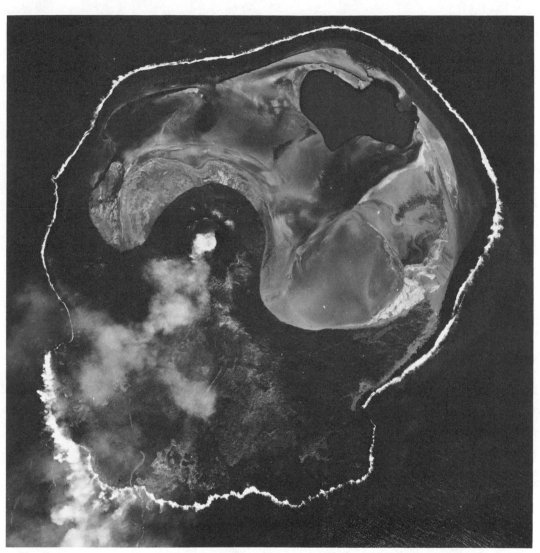

B

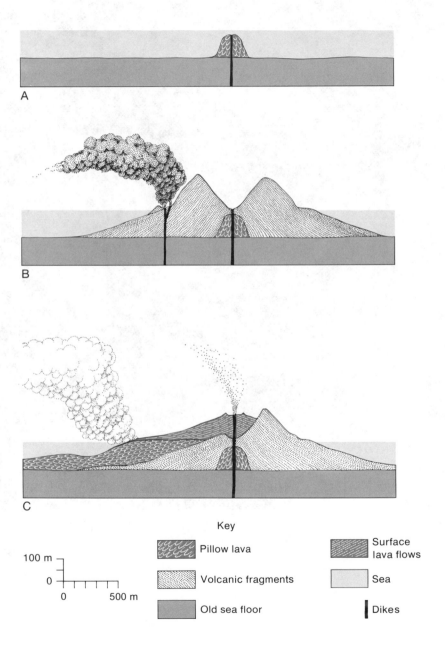

Key

⌇	Pillow lava	⬟	Surface lava flows
⠄	Volcanic fragments	▨	Sea
▨	Old sea floor	❘	Dikes

100 m

0

0   500 m

15 Diagrammatic cross sections showing the three main phases of the eruption of Surtsey: A. Submarine volcano of pillow lava, a type of lava that forms in the deep-sea environment. B. Explosive eruptions near sea level building the island of loose volcanic fragments. C. Above-sea-level eruptions of lava flows capping and armoring the island. (Adapted from Sigurdur Thorarinsson.)

In one sense the story of Surtsey is just beginning. The new island is closed to all but researchers studying the ways in which, even in this hostile environment, life takes hold and slowly but tenaciously develops a complex ecological system.

From empty sea, through chaos and barren island, to the first touch of plants and insects, the story of Surtsey recapitulates in a small way the origin of the Earth.

3
Fire under the Sea

3 Fire under the Sea

In nature things move violently to their
place, and calmly in their place.
Francis Bacon (1561–1626)

What do Surtsey and other rift volcanoes tell us about the formation of the Earth? They tell us that the entire deep ocean floor, 60 percent of the Earth's surface, is of volcanic origin—the product of rift volcanism.

The worldwide rift system is 60,000 kilometers long, and nearly all of it is submarine. Where it does appear as land in places like Iceland, the Azores, and the Galapagos Islands, the volcanic activity is probably greater than along the submarine ridges; great enough, in fact, to build the ridge above sea level. The reason for this difference in volcanic activity is a topic of lively debate, and we'll return to it in Chapter 7, Hot Spots. However, most geologists now agree that the rift islands are reasonably typical of the volcanic and structural processes that occur on the mid-ocean ridges; they are certainly easier to study.

Geologists who have studied the ocean ridges believe that a reservoir of molten rock, known as a magma chamber, exists at a depth of only 1 or 2 kilometers beneath the central rift valley. This shallow body of molten rock is only a few kilometers wide and high, but it is tens of thousands of kilometers long, stretching along the crest of all the oceanic ridges. Molten rock from this chamber feeds up into the spreading rift and thus heals the crack between the separating plates (Figure 16).

The number of volcanic eruptions that occur every year to heal this submarine crack must be more than those observed on land. Although a deep submarine volcanic eruption has never been observed, a rough estimate of the number of such events can be made from the observed average of 1 eruption every 5

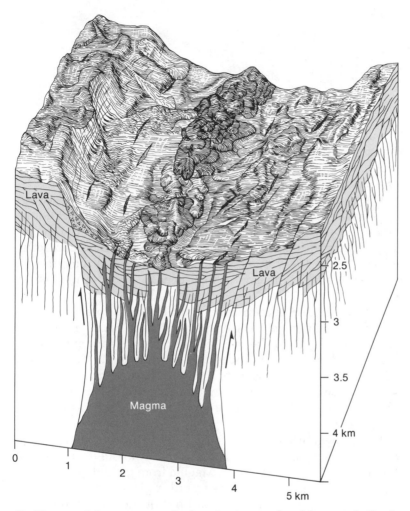

16 Diagram of the structure and submarine topography of the central rift valley of the Mid-Atlantic ridge. The vertical scale is exaggerated two times. (After R. Hekinian, J.G. Moore, and W.B. Bryan, *Contributions to Mineralogy and Petrology* 58, 1976, p. 107.)

years in Iceland. Iceland represents about 1/200 of the length of the spreading oceanic ridges. To account for its extra elevation let's assume that Iceland's eruption rate is twice that of an equal length of the submarine ridges, whose volcanoes therefore erupt once every 10 years. Thus (200 Icelands) times (1/10 of an eruption per year) equals (20 eruptions per year) along the oceanic ridge system. The fact that not one of these deep submarine eruptions has ever been witnessed, even by oceanographic instruments, shows us that many frontiers remain to be crossed in our exploration of the Earth.

The volume of volcanic rock needed to heal the scar between the spreading plates is enormous. Every year 2.5 square kilometers of new seafloor is formed by the spreading of the plates. The rocky plates are 4 or 5 kilometers thick at their spreading edges. Hence the volume of new volcanic rock amounts to about 12 cubic kilometers of new oceanic crust formed every year.

The description of the Surtsey eruption in Chapter 2 contains an interesting paradox. The eruption of molten rock from a vent at shallow depth in the sea led to violent steam explosions. However, the lava that flowed through tunnels to the growing edge of Surtsey was seen to flow beneath the waves and to generate white steam clouds without violent disruption of the molten rock. Both were fire under the sea. Why was only the former explosive?

The answer involves the amount of water and other gases dissolved in the magma, which is normally about 0.5 percent of the weight of the molten rock. Magma from great depth erupted in shallow water quickly forms a chilled glassy rind. At the low surface pressures, most gases boil out of the molten rock and greatly expand in volume. This expansion fractures the glassy rind of the venting magma and allows sea water access to a large surface of finely broken but still hot rock. The steam generated by this contact water, added to the steam and other gases boiling out from within the magma gives rise to the explosions.

Lava that has been erupted from a crater on land and has then moved through tunnels to the sea has already lost most of its dissolved gases. As it flows into the sea, it forms sacklike bodies of lava with chilled glassy rinds; these bodies are called *pillow lavas* (Figure 17). The "pillows" do not fracture from the expansion of internal gases because those gases have already boiled away on land. A relatively small surface area loses

A

B

17 Pillow lavas formed by volcanic flows under water are some of the most widespread rocks on Earth. A. Pillow lavas formed beneath the prehistoric glacial ice on Iceland. B. Young pillow lavas on the Mid-Atlantic ridge 2700 meters below the ocean surface. (Photograph taken from the submarine Alvin by W.B. Bryan of Woods Hole Oceanographic Institution.)

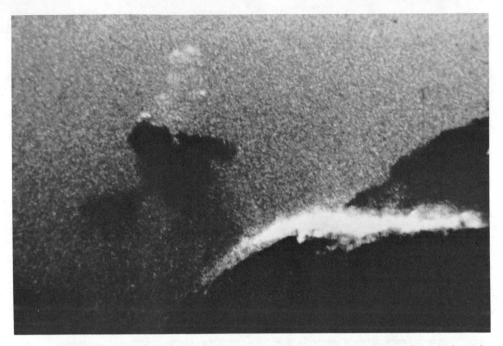

18 Diver studies the process of pillow-lava formation. The growing pillow in the right foreground is enlarging along a red-hot seam (white in this photograph). The lack of steam, even at this shallow depth, indicates there is little conduction of heat from the molten lava to the water. The lavas from Kilauea Volcano, Hawaii, entering the sea in 1971 and 1973 provided diving geologists the first opportunity to observe directly the formation of this widespread type of rock. (Photograph by Lee Tepley from the movie *Fire Under the Sea,* by Moonlight Productions, Mountain View, California.)

heat to the surrounding water, and the quiet formation of steam takes place without explosions (Figure 18).

This process suggests that lavas emitted from vents in deep water, deep enough that the dissolved gases can't boil and expand, will also quietly form pillow lavas. Because the contact water will be under too high pressure to boil, no steam will form. The violence of fire under the sea is thus controlled by depth. The common sense that fire and water are antagonistic originates in the limited view of our surface pressure environment. Of course the term fire is used loosely. In this context, fire means hot and glowing, not the combustion of a fuel with oxygen to produce flames.

The critical depth below which submarine lava is not explosive depends on the dissolved gas content and the temperature of the magma, but for all practical purposes this depth is only

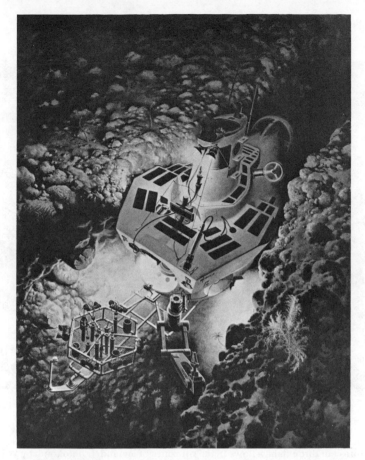

19 The submarine Alvin in the rift valley of the Mid-Atlantic ridge This artist's conception shows Alvin exploring an open fracture cutting across young pillow lavas at a depth of 2600 meters. (Painting by the National Geographic Society.)

about 30 meters below sea level. Most of the oceanic ridges where the seafloor is spreading and new oceanic crust is forming are more than 2000 meters below sea level. Pillow lavas should therefore be the pavement of the spreading seafloors. Rocks dredged from the ridges by oceanographic ships and sampled on recent dives by scientists in special submarines confirm this theory (Figure 19).

Jim Moore, one of the divers who descended 3000 meters into the valley along the crest of the Mid-Atlantic ridge, describes the scene as a strange, silent land of pillow lava hills and yawning cracks, with a dusting of sedimentary mud. The

20 View down into an open fracture in the rift valley of the Mid-Atlantic ridge. The fracture cuts across sediment-covered pillow lavas and was evidently formed by the forces separating the plates. This photo was taken at a depth of about 2700 meters during Project FAMOUS (French–American Mid-Ocean Undersea Study) in 1974. Similar above sea-level fractures cut through lava flows in the rift zones of Iceland. (Photograph by W.B. Bryan, Woods Hole Oceanographic Institution.)

pillow lavas form steep-sided hills 20 to 30 meters high and 0.5 to 1.0 kilometer wide near the center of the 4-kilometer-wide rift valley. These hills appear fresh and recently erupted; they clearly mark the very axis of the spreading oceanic ridge system.

On the valley floor on either side of the hills, many of the lavas look older. They are being covered with loose sedimentary debris which is slowly raining down from the ocean surface above. Most of the sediment is composed of microscopic shells of calcium carbonate formed by floating plants and animals. The relative age of the submarine lava flows can be established by the thickness of the sedimentary mud which slowly accumulates with time (Figure 20).

Deep cracks parallel to the rift valley cut across the older

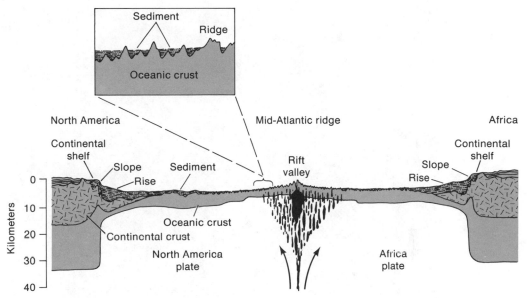

21 Cross section of the Earth beneath the Atlantic Ocean Basin. North America and Africa are both moving with the spreading seafloor, forming "passive" continental margins. Sediments accumulating in the valleys between the volcanic ridges slowly bury the rugged submarine mountains. (After B.C. Heezen, in F. Press and R. Siever, *Earth*, Second Edition, p. 262. W.H. Freeman and Company, Copyright © 1978.)

lavas. These cracks result from the pulling apart of the entire ocean ridge system. The steep walls that form the sides of the rift valley appear to be normal faults along which the valley has dropped down 500 meters relative to the ridge.

For over 1000 kilometers on either side of the rift valley, the Mid-Atlantic ridge slopes generally downward away from the ridge over rugged and fractured volcanic terrain into deep basins 4000 to 5000 meters below sea level (Figure 21).

One of the main arguments about rift volcanoes is whether they are a cause or an effect of the rifting apart of the oceanic ridges. Does the intrusion of volcanic rocks push apart the plates, or does the pulling or dragging apart of the plates form cracks through which the magma can rise to the surface? Most experts now favor the latter view, although the answer may be both.

We have been measuring the spreading in Iceland during the last ten years with sensitive surveying instruments that can

22 Aerial photograph of fractures in the rift zone of Iceland. These fractures mark the continuation of the crest of the Mid-Atlantic ridge across Iceland. The lava flows in this area are less than 6000 years old. Summer homes dot the edge of the lake formed by the central valley of the rift.

detect changes of less than a centimeter over distances of 5 kilometers. The results of this study indicate that the rift zones slowly widen and sink a few millimeters per year across distances of 10 to 30 kilometers, without earthquakes or volcanic eruptions. When the tensional strain reaches the breaking point, the rift fractures (Figure 22).

A rifting event takes place in a few hours or days. Open cracks form parallel to the rift, earthquake swarms jolt the local area, and lava erupts from some of the fissures.

We were lucky enough to be in northern Iceland when one of these rifting episodes occurred on September 7, 1977. An earthquake swarm was followed in rapid succession by a brief but spectacular volcanic fissure eruption and ground cracking parallel to the rift. In a zone about 2 kilometers across and 20 kilometers long, the cracking formed open fractures up to 20 centimeters wide with vertical offsets as large as one meter. All this occurred between 3 PM and midnight (Figure 23).

23 A gaping fracture formed during an earthquake swarm in northern Iceland on September 7, 1977. This rifting event was related to an eruption of Krafla Volcano. The cone in the background was formed in a prehistoric eruption of Krafla.

One of the cracks cut through a producing geothermal steam field. Some magma must have been injected along this fracture, for one of the steam wells erupted brief spurts of incandescent lava. The erupting lava cut through the heavy metal pipe at the well head and showered a few tons of frothy lava fragments around the well. This is the only known case where lava has erupted from a man-made vent (Figure 24).

One survey line about 4 kilometers long that crossed the fracture zone lengthened more than 1 meter. Survey lines on the flanks of the new fracture zone showed contraction. The picture of rifting that emerges is one of slow stretching for 100 to 200 years over a wide zone, followed by rupture that concentrates the deformation into a narrow central zone and allows the flanks to contract back to an unstretched condition. It's like pulling a rubber band slowly and then cutting it in the middle; all the stretching that had slowly accumulated is suddenly concentrated in the cut, and the sides contract. Perhaps a sudden tear in a piece of elastic cloth when it is slowly stretched would be a better analogy since its dimensions fit the plates more closely than does a rubber band.

The length of the tear in a rifting episode is 10 to 100 kilometers long, only a very small fraction of the length of the entire rift system. The rifting episodes are infrequent in any one place, perhaps only once every few hundred years. However, at any given time somewhere over the entire length of the ocean ridge system rifting is probably occurring.

The presence of magma under pressure beneath the rift zones probably aids the rupture process just as a wedge speeds the felling of a leaning tree. The processes of rifting and volcanism are so interrelated that it is difficult to sort out cause and effect—reminding us of Samuel Butler's remark that "a hen is just an egg's way of making another egg."

There is no doubt, however, that great chains of volcanoes, mostly submarine, circle the Earth in several belts along the crests of the oceanic ridges. They owe their origin to the still mysterious forces that spread the plates. Surtsey is only a visible tip of this vast hidden activity.

24 Incandescent lava was briefly ejected from this geothermal steam well in Iceland during the eruption of Krafla Volcano on September 7, 1977. A fracture somewhere between the surface and the 1200-meter depth of the well broke the well casing and allowed a small amount of molten rock to enter the producing well. The steam lifted the magma spray to the surface where it melted and abraded its way through the pipe. The few tons of small lava bombs that were ejected form the granular surface material. This is the only known case of a volcanic vent produced by drilling.

Opposite. Anak Krakatau in 1960.

4
Krakatau, West of Java

4 Krakatau, West of Java

Had the fierce ashes of some fiery peak
Been hurl'd so high they ranged about the globe?
For day by day, thro' many a blood-red eve,
The wrathful sunset glared. . .
Tennyson (1809–1892)

Most of our present mountains, valleys, and plains have been slowly sculptured by erosion over the last million years, and these in turn have formed from other landscapes long vanished. Volcanoes, though, operate on a different time scale.

Krakatau, alias Krakatoa, disgorged 18 cubic kilometers of rock, produced tidal waves over 30 meters high, and formed a circular depression 6 kilometers in diameter and 1 kilometer deep (called a *caldera*) in less than one day. In that short time, Krakatau erupted more volcanic rock than is formed along all the oceanic rifts in one year. The Earth does evolve slowly, but much of the change is the sum of many catastrophic moments.

The explosion of Krakatau in 1883 produced worldwide effects. The noise was heard for thousands of kilometers, and the shock wave recorded on barographs around the world. The dust that was lifted into the stratosphere circled the globe producing astonishing visual effects: colorful sunrises and sunsets and a blue-green appearance of the sun and moon. The dust spread westward, encircling the equator in two weeks, then drifted both north and south. Average solar radiation in Europe decreased 10 percent over the next 3 years, and average world temperatures were below normal.

As attention from many fields focused on the eruption and its aftermath, scientists came to realize the worldwide interdependence of land, sea, and air.

Krakatau is a small group of uninhabited volcanic islands in the Sunda Straits between Java and Sumatra, on a main oceanic trade route between Europe and the Orient. There had not been an eruption there since 1680. The highest peak on the islands was less than 1000 meters tall; it was not an imposing cone.

On May 20, 1883 Krakatau began to erupt with small explosions of ash from a low crater on the north end of the main island. Dutch scientists visited the island on May 27 and noted that much of the vegetation had been killed but not burned by the accumulation of fine volcanic ash. Some blocks of pumice, a rock composed of glassy froth so filled with bubble holes that it floats on water, were also noticed.

The activity declined until late June, when passing ships reported two columns of steam. Apparently a new vent had also become active. On August 11 the island was again visited. Three vents were producing small explosive eruptions, but not much additional ash had accumulated since May, and some trees were still alive on the southern peak of the island.

Things changed on August 26. At 1 PM noises like thunder were heard up to 200 kilometers away, and by 2 PM a black cloud had climbed to 27 kilometers over Krakatau. The closest witnesses were aboard the British ship Charles Bal, bound for Hong Kong (Figure 25). The captain's log gives some vivid impressions of the climax of the eruption.

> (August 26) At noon, wind west-south-west, weather fine, the Island of Krakatoa to the northeast of us, but only a small portion of the northeast point, close to the water, showing; rest of the island covered with a dense black cloud. At 2:30 PM noticed some agitation about the Point of Krakatoa; clouds or something being propelled with amazing velocity to the northeast. To us it looked like blinding rain, and had the appearance of a furious squall of ashen hue. At once shortened sail to topsails and foresail. At 5 PM the roaring noise continued and increased, darkness spread over the sky, and a hail of pumice stone fell on us, many pieces being of considerable size and quite warm. Had to cover up the skylights to save the glass, while feet and head had to be protected with boots and southwesters. About 6 PM the fall of larger stones ceased, but there continued a steady fall of a smaller kind, most blinding to the eyes, and covering the decks with 3 to 4 inches very speedily, while an intense blackness covered the sky and

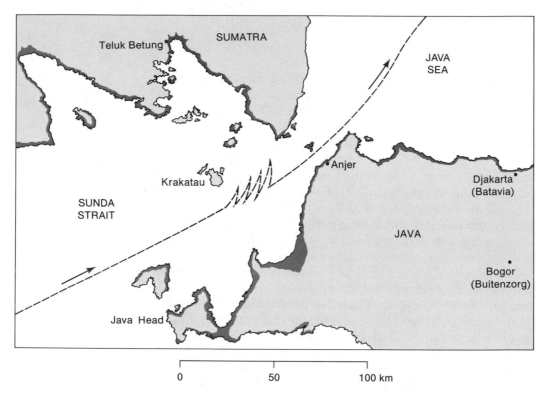

25 Path of the sailing ship Charles Bal during the eruption of Krakatau is shown by the broken line. The shaded areas on the coasts of Java and Sumatra were the zones inundated by tsunamis (tidal waves) from the giant explosive eruptions and caldera collapse. (After C.J. Symons, ed., *The Eruption of Krakatoa.* Royal Society Report of the Krakatoa Committee, 1888.)

land and sea. Sailed on our course until we got what we thought was a sight of Fourth Point Light; then brought the ship to the wind, southwest, as we could not see any distance, and we knew not what might be in the Straits, the night being a fearful one. The blinding fall of sand and stones, the intense blackness above and around us, broken only by the incessant glare of varied kinds of lightning and the continued explosive roar of Krakatoa, made our situation a truly awful one. At 11 PM, having stood off from the Java shore, wind strong from the southwest, the island, eleven miles west-north-west, became more visible, chains of fire appearing to ascend and descend between the sky and it, while on the southwest end there seemed to be a continued roll of balls of

white fire; the wind, though strong, was hot and choking, sulphurous, with a smell like burning cinders. From midnight to 4 AM the same inpenetrable darkness continuing, the roaring of Krakatoa less continuous but more explosive in sound, the sky one second intense blackness and the next a blaze of fire; mastheads and yardarms studded with electrical glows and a peculiar pinky flame coming from clouds which seemed to touch the mastheads and yardarms. At 6 AM, being able to make out the Java shore, set sail. Passed Anjer at 8:30 AM, close enough in to make out the houses, but could see no movement of any kind. At 11:15 there was a fearful explosion in the direction of Krakatoa, now over 30 miles distant. We saw a wave rush right on to Button Island, apparently sweeping right over the south part and rising half way up the north and east sides. This we saw repeated twice, but the helmsman says he saw it once before we looked. The same waves seemed also to run right on to the Java shore. The sky rapidly covered in, by 11:30 AM we were inclosed in a darkness that might almost be felt. At the same time commenced a downpour of mud, sand, and I know not what; ship going northeast by north, seven knots under three lower topsails; put out the side lights, placed two men on the lookout forward, while mate and second mate looked out on either quarter, and one man employed washing the mud off binnacle glass. We had seen two vessels to the north and northwest of us before the sky closed in, adding much to the anxiety of our position. At noon the darkness was so intense that we had to grope about the decks, and although speaking to each other on the poop, yet could not see each other. This horrible state and downpour of mud continued until 1:30 PM, the roarings of the volcano and lightnings being something fearful. By 2 PM we could see the yards aloft, and the fall of mud ceased. Up to midnight the sky hung dark and heavy, a little sand falling at times, the roaring of the volcano very distinct although we were fully sixty-five or seventy miles northeast from it. Such darkness and time of it few would conceive, and many, I dare say, would disbelieve. The ship, from truck to waterline, is as if cemented; spars, sails, blocks, and ropes in a terrible mess; but, thank God, nobody hurt or ship damaged. On the other hand, how fares it with Anjer, Merak, and the other little villages on the Java coast?
(*Nature*, Vol. 29, 1883, pp. 140–141.)

Not well. Over 36,000 people had been drowned by the great tidal waves generated by the major explosion and collapse. The tidal waves were the real catastrophe of Krakatau. Ships in the area were not swamped, but slowly rode up and down with the swells whose crests and troughs were kilometers apart. But as these waves reached shallow water, particularly in the bays that faced Krakatau, they began to curl and break, forming huge surf waves that swept inland and swamped everything in their reach. In some locations where they were channeled into narrowing bays they rose to over 30 meters above sea level.

The 10 AM explosion was the largest natural concussion ever recorded. The ash cloud rose to 80 kilometers above Krakatau, and the detonation was heard in Australia. The main tidal wave swept the coasts of Java and Sumatra about half an hour after the explosion (Figure 26).

At 10:50 AM a second huge explosion occurred but apparently this one did not generate tidal waves. Throughout the afternoon and night of August 27 explosions of diminishing intensity recurred and finally ceased. A few small eruptions continued into September and October, but most of the violence was packed into the time between 1 PM August 26 and 11 AM August 27.

The Sunda Straits were choked with floating pumice. As ships began to make their way through, sailors soon noticed that most of Krakatau was missing. Where the peak of Danan had reached 450 meters high, there was ocean 200 meters deep. A 5- by 8-kilometer chunk of the main island had disappeared, and a curving cliff, 800 meters high, cut through the south peak down to sea level. The origin of this caldera has been a major subject of debate ever since the 1883 eruption (Figures 27 and 28).

Some thought the island had simply blown its top and the debris had scattered into blocks and ashes. However, over 90 percent of the erupted material was pumice of a texture and composition not found in the wreck of the old volcano. It must have come from the magma chamber beneath the volcano; when the volcano had emptied this chamber, the top collapsed into the void below. The great tidal waves were probably generated by the collapse that followed the largest explosion.

Most geologists now believe that calderas are largely formed by collapse. These great circular basins, up to 20 kilometers in diameter, are common volcanic features and attest to even greater eruptions than Krakatau in prehistoric times.

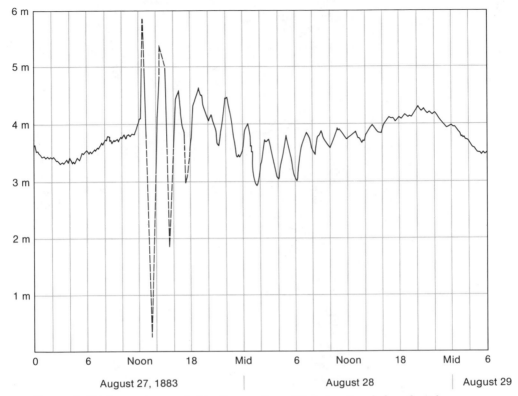

26 Tsunamis (tidal waves) generated by the eruption of Krakatau recorded on the tide gauge at Djakarta (Batavia in 1883), 170 kilometers from the source, August 27–29, 1883. The broken lines are off scale, but reconstructed from high-water marks and eyewitness accounts. (After Symons, 1888.)

The Krakatau pumice covered thousands of square kilometers and is calculated to have a volume of 18 cubic kilometers. The volume of island that had disappeared was about 6 cubic kilometers; the difference can be explained by the fact that expanded pumice has three times the volume of its solid rock equivalent.

Some students of Krakatau have proposed that the sea water was important in generating the explosions, as was the case at Surtsey. However, the expansion of the pumice into a frothy glass is so complete throughout the scattered blocks that the

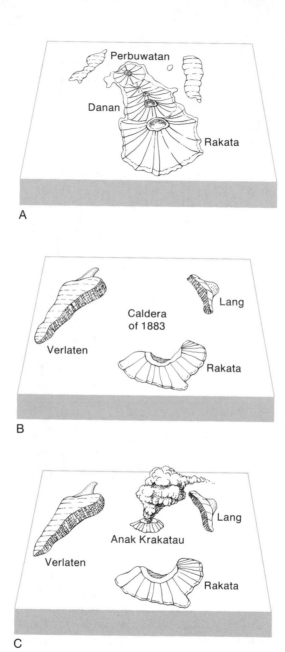

27 Changes at Krakatau since 1880. A. Krakatau before 1883. B. Krakatau after the 1883 eruption. C. Krakatau today. Before the eruption, Rakata Peak was about 800 meters high, and the main island about 9 kilometers long. Anak Krakatau, the presently active island, began with submarine eruptions in 1927.

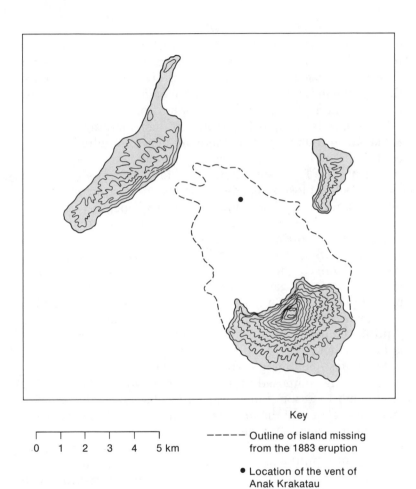

Key

```
|---|---|---|---|---|
0   1   2   3   4   5 km
```

- - - - - Outline of island missing
from the 1883 eruption

● Location of the vent of
Anak Krakatau

28 Sketch map of the Krakatau Islands after the great 1883 eruption. The missing area is 23 square kilometers; where a volcanic peak 450 meters high once stood, the water is now 275 meters deep.

expanding gases must have come from within the erupting rock. A high content of dissolved water in the magma rather than contact steam appears to have propelled the explosions. Crater Lake in Oregon and many other calderas have formed by explosion and collapse in locations far from the sea.

The deposits of explosive debris on the remaining islands of Krakatau surrounding the caldera are tens to hundreds of meters thick. The lower layers are distinct and composed of well-sorted pumice fragments, indicating fallout from an eruption cloud. Each explosion makes a separate and distinct layer. The debris from the two final huge explosions is poorly sorted and only vaguely layered. Pumice and fine ash were produced so rapidly that no sorting took place. The deposits were emplaced as great glowing avalanches of fine and coarse volcanic fragments all mixed together. No lava flows were formed. The rapid expansion of gas in the magma formed the pumice lumps by cooling the molten glass to solid but still hot and glowing fragments. The pumice, fine ash, and escaping gases form a fluidlike emulsion, much like a snow avalanche except that it is fiercely hot.

These fast-moving glowing avalanches, known as *nuées ardentes,* are composed of newly erupted volcanic debris and are the most awesome and destructive of all volcanic phenomena. Huge clouds of the finer ash fragments are lifted above the glowing avalanches by the heat and turbulence. This finer material, sometimes mixed with rain, falls out over large areas downwind from the eruption as volcanic ash or mud.

Australians 4800 kilometers away heard the largest Krakatau explosion as the sound of cannon firing. The shock wave rattled doors and broke windows in west Java, and was recorded on barographs around the Earth. The more sensitive instruments recorded 2 or 3 world-circling trips of the air wave, each circuit taking about 36 hours. The 58-megaton nuclear test in the atmosphere over northern Russia in 1961 produced similar world-circling air-pressure waves.

It is popular to compare the powers of nature with man-made explosions, but this is often misleading. The thermal energy in

29 Aerial view of Anak Krakatau in June 1959. Rakata Island and the 1883 caldera wall are in the background.

the 18 cubic kilometers of hot material erupted by Krakatau is equal to that of nearly 5000 megatons of hydrogen bombs. However, only about 5 percent of the Krakatau thermal energy was converted to mechanical energy and its release was spread out over a day's time, in contrast to the almost instant release of energy in a nuclear bomb. Even so, it is somewhat reassuring that nature can still unleash more raw energy than that in man's biggest bomb.

Quiet prevailed at Krakatau for 44 years; then small explosive submarine eruptions began on the north rim of the caldera in 1927. Soon a small cinder cone was built above sea level; it was named Anak Krakatau—child of Krakatau. This small island has had a fitful history over the past 50 years, sometimes growing during periods of small ash and cinder explosions, and sometimes being nearly washed away by waves from the Indian Ocean (Figure 29).

In 1960 we visited the new island during an eruptive episode. Small explosions of fragments from fine ash up to 2-meter blocks were occurring at 30-second to 10-minute intervals. These explosions formed turbulent ash clouds rising from 150 to 1200 meters above the 1.5-kilometer-diameter island. Krakatau is in a rebuilding phase, but it's in no rush compared to 1883. The volume of the new island is only about 0.5 cubic kilometer (Figure 30).

Since 1960, lava flows have issued from the crater and formed a protective cap on the island. The growth of Anak Krakatau has been similar to the formation of Surtsey. The lavas retard wave erosion and give the new Krakatau a slightly more permanent place in a notoriously impermanent part of the world.

Will Krakatau ever erupt as violently again? Probably not for many thousands of years. The present composition of the lava indicates that most of the highly explosive magma was expelled in 1883, and new magma of this type forms slowly. However, other volcanoes on the Ring of Fire may be approaching the stage of Krakatau in 1883. Calderas are a common volcanic feature and new ones can be expected to form every few centuries.

30 Moderate explosive eruption of Anak Krakatau in January 1960, forming a 1000-meter-high ash cloud. The energy released in this explosion is less than one-millionth of the energy of the 1883 eruption.

Opposite. Cerro Negro Volcano, Nicaragua, 1968.

5
Ring of Fire

5 Ring of Fire

Far away, shrouded in fog we saw the silhouettes
of the volcanic islands—links in
Pluto's mighty chain.
Y. Markhinin   (1971)

America is drifting away from Europe, but it is also drifting toward Japan. In fact, all the plates around the Pacific are slowly converging along subduction zones that encircle this vast ocean. Volcanoes related to these converging plate margins form a ring of fire that nearly surrounds the Pacific Basin.

Krakatau is located on the island arc of Indonesia, between the converging Australian and Asian plates. Mount Fuji is on the subduction zone that forms the Japanese island arcs between the Asian and Pacific plates. Volcanoes in the Kamchatka Peninsula of the Soviet Union, Alaska, the northwestern United States, Mexico, Central America, the Andes, New Zealand, New Guinea, and the Philippines complete the circuit (Figure 31).

Subduction zones generate about 400 of the 500 known active volcanoes in the world; that is, those which have erupted at least once in historic time. The Mediterranean volcanoes of Italy and Greece are included in this tally.

There are major differences between subduction volcanoes and rift volcanoes. Subduction volcanoes form island arcs and high mountain chains rather than submarine ridges; they are more explosive and produce large volumes of ash as well as lava flows; their products are more variable in composition; even their basic shapes as individual mountains differ from those formed at extensional margins.

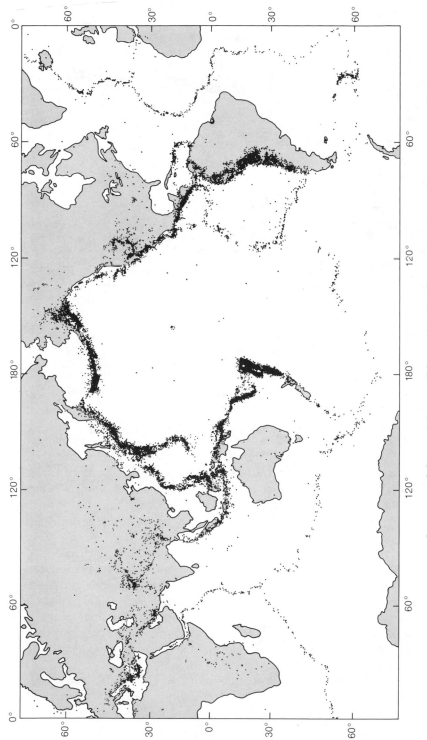

31 Ring of Fire around the Pacific Ocean, delineated by locations of earthquakes occurring between 1963 and 1977 with a magnitude greater than 4.5, as determined by the U.S. Geological Survey's National Earthquake Information Service. (Map plotted by the Environmental Data and Information Service of the National Oceanic and Atmospheric Administration.)

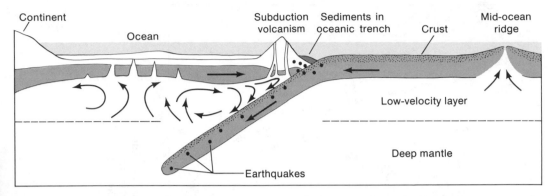

32 Plate of crust and solid upper mantle formed at the Mid-Ocean Ridge moves on the plastic low-velocity layer and is thrust beneath a converging plate at a subduction zone. An oceanic trench forms where the plates converge, and an island arc of compressed rocks and volcanoes forms over the downgoing plate. (From M. Nafi Toksoz, "The Subduction of the Lithosphere." Copyright © 1975 by Scientific American, Inc. All rights reserved.)

Rift volcanoes are located at the exact edges of the separating plates. In contrast, subduction volcanoes occur about 100 to 200 kilometers landward from the deep ocean trenches that mark the compressional edges of converging plates.

Chains of subduction volcanoes form graceful arcs a few thousand kilometers in length across the globe. A close look shows that 5 or 10 volcanoes often form a fairly straight line a few hundred kilometers in length, with a slight bend or offset between adjoining groups. The bends between the groups form the overall arc, which is generally convex toward the open ocean side.

Japan is a good example of a subduction chain, with about 50 volcanoes along parts of 4 arcs. The deep-sea trenches lie 200 kilometers on the Pacific Ocean side of the volcanoes and mark the actual boundary between the Pacific and Asian plates. A region of earthquakes dips from near the Earth's surface at the trenches beneath the island arcs. This region roughly outlines the upper surface of the Pacific plate as it plunges beneath the Asian plate.

The belt of volcanoes occurs on the overlying plate where the earthquake zone is 100 to 200 kilometers beneath the Earth's surface (Figure 32). Most of the large volcanoes are on the eastern edge of this belt where the earthquake zone is shallower. Japanese geologists refer to this eastern edge as the volcanic front. The number of volcanoes and their production of volcanic rocks decreases gradually with distance away from the volcanic front, toward Asia, but stops abruptly on the Pacific side of the volcanic front.

This setting is generally characteristic of all subduction zone volcanoes, and indicates that magma is being generated when the descending plate sinks to a depth of 100 to 200 kilometers. Most Japanese geologists believe that frictional heating of the descending plate contributes to the production of magma. This hypothesis best explains the sudden onset of the volcanic front. The gradual decrease in volcanism behind the volcanic front is explained by the fact that there is more chance for magma to cool on the longer ascent to the surface.

Another reason why magma is generated during subduction is that the sinking plate drags down sediments and oceanic crust which contain water. Water lowers the melting temperature of magma. The presence of water also explains the higher gas content and greater explosiveness of subduction volcanoes.

Once enough magma has formed at sufficient depth, the greater density of the surrounding rocks exerts an upward force on the magma. Its ascent toward the surface may be aided by fractures in the overlying plate. The distance between volcanoes in island arcs is usually about 50 to 70 kilometers. This spacing is about the thickness of the overlying plate, which is reasonable because the spacing of fractures in a rigid plate resting on a soft layer tends to be about the same as the thickness of the plate.

The silica content of most rift volcanoes is about 50 percent and varies only a few percentage points, while the silica content of subduction volcanoes varies from about 50 to 70 percent. The silica content largely determines which minerals form in volcanic rocks and thereby controls the nature of the mineral deposits and sediments associated with the volcanic rocks. For example, the mineral quartz (SiO_2) does not form until the silica content of rocks exceeds 55 percent. In Iceland there is no quartz in the lavas, there are no white, sandy beaches with quartz grains, and there are no quartz veins containing precious metal deposits. On the Ring of Fire, however, the volcanic rocks usually contain quartz grains which erode to form quartz sand beaches; and gold, silver, and copper mines pock the eroded stumps of older volcanoes.

The composition of volcanic rocks is controlled by three major factors: partial melting processes, partial crystallization processes, and contamination by surrounding rocks.

Partial melting is the process by which part of the solid upper mantle of the Earth is turned into magma. Rocks are a mixture of several chemical compounds, and these do not all have the same melting points. In a partial melt, the first fraction to melt will have a larger proportion of the low-melting-point compounds than the parent rock. An analogy is the extraction of alcohol from hard cider by freezing and thawing. If a completely frozen block of hard cider is slowly melted, the first fraction to melt contains a higher proportion of alcohol than does the remaining solid block.

Partial crystallization is just the opposite. As a molten rock slowly cools, compounds with higher melting points crystallize first and the residual melt keeps changing in composition. This is analogous to slowly freezing the hard cider and thereby concentrating the alcohol in the residual unfrozen liquid.

Silica is concentrated in the low-melting-point fractions, especially when water is present. Therefore, both partial melting with small quantities of water present and partial crystallization during the ascent of magma to the surface can increase the silica content of the resulting volcanic rocks.

Magma appears to ascend a much greater distance in subduction volcanoes than in rift volcanoes. Also, the magma supplying subduction volcanoes often must rise through ancient continental rocks, already high in silica, which greatly increases their chance of contamination.

These concepts of partial melting, partial freezing, and contamination all provide general explanations of the origin of the many diverse volcanic rocks. Several specific explanations have also been proposed, and the arguments favoring one process over another wax and wane on subtle details. The problem

33 Mount Fuji, or Fuji-san, the archetypal volcano. The classic shape of this nearly perfect cone with graceful concave slopes, and its location near Tokyo make it the world's best-known volcano. It rises to 3776 meters from a 30-kilometer-diameter base almost at sea level. Fuji-san embodies the beauty, majesty, and power of all nature. (Woodblock print by Hokusai 1760–1849 from his famous series, Thirty-Six Views of Mount Fuji.)

is not a lack of explanation, but too many explanations. In fact, more than one process of variation is probably at work. Truth is often a mixture of conflicting opinions.

The greater proportion of water dissolved in the magma of subduction volcanoes, coupled with slightly lower eruption temperatures than in rift volcanoes, leads to more explosive eruptions. The gas wants out, and the less hot and therefore more viscous lava retards its escape, resulting in explosive eruptions of volcanic ash. Subduction eruptions often begin with explosive showers of ash, cinders, and blocks and terminate with thick, viscous lava flows. Such alternations of volcanic ash and lava flows build steep beautiful cones like Mount Fuji, the archetype of classic volcanic form (Figure 33).

Ten to fifteen subduction volcanoes erupt every year. A few, like Stromboli in the Mediterranean, have been in nearly continuous eruption for centuries. Others have erupted only once in historic time. In general, the longer the period between eruptions, the greater the likelihood that an eruption will be a major one. The products of subduction volcanoes are largely explosive: ash, pumice, cinders, blocks, and molten lava bombs. This is in sharp contrast to the rift volcanoes along the ocean ridges whose products are mainly effusive (nonexplosive) lava flows. The more notorious of the world's volcanoes belong to the subduction clan: Vesuvius, Pelée, Katmai, Bezymianny, and of course Krakatau.

Vesuvius buried Pompeii in 79 A.D. and provided a time capsule of Roman art, architecture, and artifacts for its nineteenth and twentieth-century excavators. Vesuvius was considered extinct before its violent eruption in Roman times. It has had many eruptions since then, the latest in 1944 (Figure 34).

Mont Pelée in the West Indies annihilated the 28,000 inhabitants of the port of Saint Pierre on May 8, 1902. A glowing avalanche, or nuée ardente, rushed down the mountainside and the hot gases and ash bowled over and burned everything in their path, including ships in the harbor. The disaster took only a few minutes and left just two survivors in Saint Pierre (Figure 35).

Katmai erupted on the Alaska Peninsula for two days in June 1912. The ash fall totaled 20 cubic kilometers and practically buried Kodiak Island. A caldera 5 kilometers wide engulfed Katmai Peak, and 10 cubic kilometers of glowing avalanche deposits filled a valley 20 kilometers long and 3 kilometers wide to form the Valley of Ten Thousand Smokes.

Bezymianny on the Kamchatka Peninsula of Siberia erupted for the first time in recorded history on October 22, 1955 and culminated in a giant explosive eruption on March 30, 1956. The main eruption cloud reached 45 kilometers in height; large rocks were hurled 25 kilometers; a caldera 2 kilometers wide was formed; and nuées ardentes created a 3-cubic-kilometer

34 Pompeii was buried beneath 6 meters of volcanic ash for nearly two thousand years. Its destroyer and preserver, Mount Vesuvius, is in the background. Airfall ash and nuées ardentes buried the town in one day in 79 A.D. Pliny, a Roman Historian, described the eruption cloud as looking like a pine tree; a puzzling comparison until you note the tree behind the ruins.

deposit that Russian geologists call the Valley of Ten Thousand Smokes of Kamchatka (Figure 36). Fortunately at both Katmai and Bezymianny the area was almost uninhabited and no one was killed. Such eruptions in Japan, or Central America, or anywhere on the Ring of Fire where populations are dense would have been catastrophic.

Radiocarbon dating of charred trees buried by enormous glowing avalanche deposits shows that even larger volcanic explosions once wracked the Ring of Fire. Volumes of lava

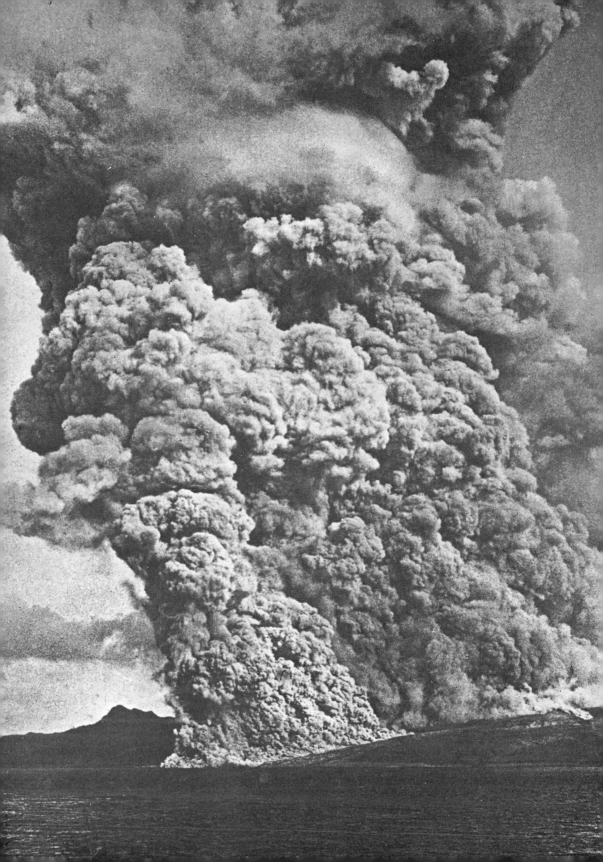

35 *Opposite.* Large nuée ardente eruption from Mont Pelée, several months after a similar cloud of hot gases and volcanic ash destroyed Saint-Pierre and killed 28,000 people within minutes. (Photograph by A. Lacroix in 1902, courtesy of the American Museum of Natural History.)

more than ten times greater than that hurled from Krakatau have been spewed forth in single eruptions. The message of such gigantic eruptions isn't imminent doom; they don't occur that often. To us their message is attention and respect; since the millions of people who reside on the Ring of Fire must live with these volcanic eruptions, it makes sense to try to understand them better.

36 Giant explosion cloud from Bezymianny Volcano, Kamchatka, March 30, 1956. The lower edge of the huge fan-shaped ash cloud is about 7 kilometers high and the top is about 35 kilometers high. (Photograph by I.V. Erov from 45 kilometers west of the volcano.)

6
Kilauea, Hawaii

6 Kilauea, Hawaii

The marriage of Pele, goddess of earth and fire,
and Kamapuaa, god of water, was short and violent.
In a rage she routed him from her crater of fire
and chased him with streams of lava into the sea.
Hawaiian legend

Kilauea Volcano on the Island of Hawaii, known also as the Big Island, is the most thoroughly studied volcano in the world. It is also one of the most active, with many eruptions and glowing lava lakes that stir and boil for years at a time. Almost all its eruptions are relatively quiet outpourings of fluid lavas. The word quiet can be misleading, though, for the vents often spurt fire fountains of incandescent lava several hundred meters high, which fall into lava ponds or feed lava flows. These outpourings of lava are quiet only in contrast to explosive volcanic eruptions, which produce fragmental debris and look more like huge detonations of dynamite.

Effusive eruptions of the Hawaiian type are comparatively safe to study at close range, and the Hawaiian Volcano Observatory has been at it since 1912.

One of the most spectacular eruptions of Kilauea took place in 1959–1960. This eruption was minutely recorded by sensitive instruments and closely observed by geologists on the scene. Detailed study of the data collected led to important insights on how volcanoes erupt. Jerry Eaton and Don Richter, scientists at the Hawaiian Volcano Observatory, saw it all happen. We were in Hawaii both before and after, but missed the eruption, thus the following description is mainly their story.

A bright orange cloud suddenly lit the night over Kilauea Iki crater, 4 kilometers east of the Observatory, at 8:08 PM on November 14, 1959. The Observatory is perched on the west rim of Kilauea caldera, a large 3-by-5-kilometer bowl on the nearly flat summit of Kilauea Volcano. Kilauea Iki, the site of the eruption, is a subsidiary crater on the opposite side of the summit caldera, separated from it by a low ridge.

The real beginning of the eruption took place almost unnoticed months before and kilometers beneath the actual outbreak. It was first indicated by a slight shifting of a sensitive tiltmeter that had been installed near the Observatory in 1957. A tiltmeter is like a giant carpenter's level, several meters long. Slight changes in water level between the ends register tilts in the Earth's surface as small as 1 millimeter over a distance of 1 kilometer. Additional tiltmeters constructed around the summit of Kilauea in 1958 and 1959 showed that the whole caldera region was bulging upward and tilting outward. Analysis of the pattern of tiltmeters indicated that magma was welling up from a great depth and accumulating in a zone a few kilometers beneath the summit.

Following several small earthquakes southeast of the caldera in February 1959, the swelling stopped. Then a swarm of 2500 microearthquakes and seismic tremor, a more continuous humming of the ground detectable only by the seismographs, began in August. The quakes originated about 55 kilometers beneath the north rim of the caldera. With this episode, magma started moving up through the deep volcanic conduits again, and rapid inflation of the summit of Kilauea resumed.

In September, a swarm of shallow microearthquakes began near Halemaumau, the inner crater of the caldera and the usual site of summit eruptions. Over 22,000 of these tiny quakes were recorded prior to the eruption. As the number of microearthquakes increased so did the rate of outward tilting, and the Observatory staff began to check its special eruption equipment just in case. They were not disappointed.

Minutes after the first glow was sighted, they were at the rim of Kilauea Iki. Fire fountains had started from a vent halfway

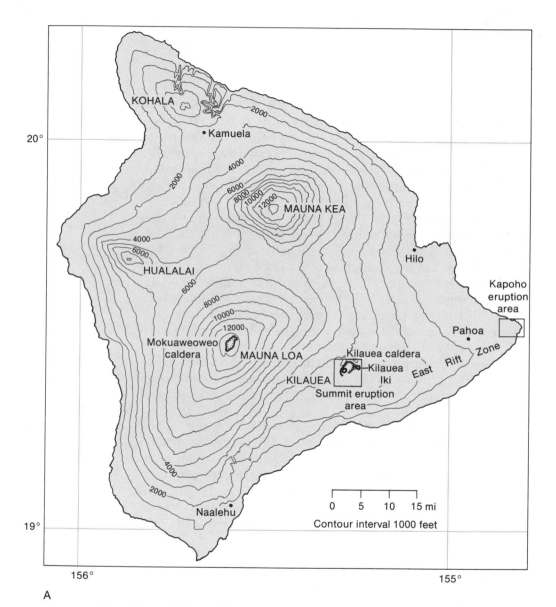

37 A. Island of Hawaii showing its five volcanoes. The insets show the location of the Kilauea Iki and Kapoho eruptions. (Map by the U.S. Geological Survey.) B. Map of Kilauea caldera and Kilauea Iki crater. The main vent of the November–December 1959 eruption was at the west end of Kilauea Iki crater. Lava ponded in the old crater to form a lava lake while falling fragments from the fire fountains built the cinder cone and elongated area of airfall deposits in the lee of the prevailing trade winds. (Map by the U.S. Geological Survey.)

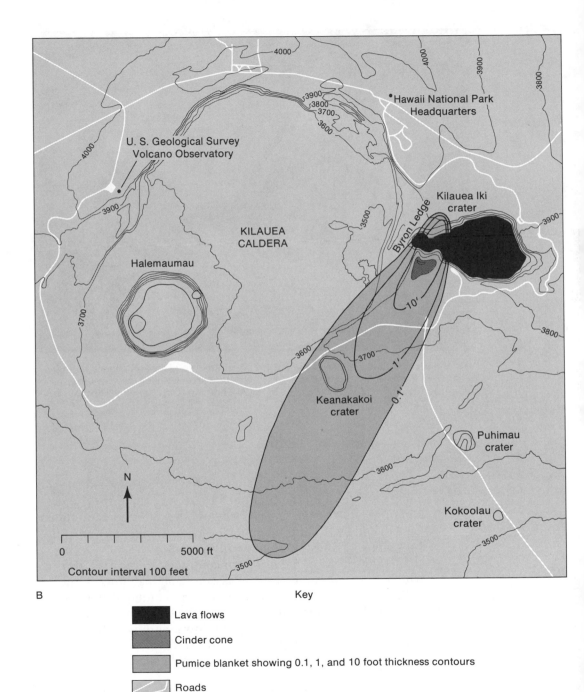

U. S. Geological Survey
Volcano Observatory

KILAUEA
CALDERA

Halemaumau

Hawaii National Park
Headquarters

Kilauea Iki
crater

Byron Ledge

10'

1'

0.1'

Keanakakoi
crater

Puhimau
crater

Kokoolau
crater

N

0   5000 ft

Contour interval 100 feet

B

Key

Lava flows

Cinder cone

Pumice blanket showing 0.1, 1, and 10 foot thickness contours

Roads

38 Fountaining lava forms a curtain of fire along the south wall of Kilauea Iki crater. Lava from the fire fountains cascades down into the 200-meter-deep crater and begins to pond on the crater floor. (Photograph by W.W. Dunmire, U.S. National Park Service.)

up the 200-meter-high south wall of the crater, and had spread along an extending fracture until by 10 PM they formed a curtain of fire 800 meters long. Gradually the outermost fountains waned, and by the afternoon of November 15 only one erupting vent along the fissure remained (Figure 38).

The first phase of the eruption continued for a week, during which every possible study was conducted. Pumice samples falling from the fire fountain and lava samples dipped with long-handled ladles from the flows were collected daily. Gases were sampled from the vents and flows, and even from fume clouds by planes flying through them. Temperature measurements were taken frequently, and portable seismographs were set up in an attempt to follow the underground movements of magma. Tape recordings were made of the awesome sounds from the gushing fire fountain and falling pumice. The rate of lava production was estimated by measuring the height of the fire fountain, which reached 600 meters during one phase of the eruption. The rise of the lava level as it ponded in the bottom of Kilauea Iki crater also provided an accurate measure of the rate of lava production. It was fortunate the vent was on the side of the crater, since this channeled most of the lava from the fountains and flows into the old crater which then served as a giant measuring bowl (Figure 39).

After a brief pause, fire fountains and flows resumed and the lava lake rose until it covered the main vent. After this phase, lava drained back down the vent from which it came until the lava lake was lowered to the level of the vent (Figures 40 and 41). Seventeen phases of eruption interrupted by these periods of drainback took place during 37 days of activity. The temperature of erupting lava varied from 1120°C to 1190°C. The maximum rate of eruption was about 1.0 million cubic meters per hour and the rate of drainback sometimes exceeded 1.5 million cubic meters per hour. These are huge amounts; enough to fill a city block 100 meters deep in an hour. The silica content of the lava varied from 46 to 50 percent and averaged about 47 percent, forming a black rock called basalt, typical of the bedrock foundation of the entire Hawaiian Island chain.

Each time the lava erupted the tiltmeters showed some deflation of the summit of Kilauea, and during drainback the summit would inflate again. The delicate balance between the erupted lava and the shallow magma chamber beneath the summit indicated that gas expansion was the main force driving the fire fountains. As lava nears the surface, the dissolved gas begins to boil out. This sudden increase in volume shoots the lava up into the fiery fountains. When the gas has been expelled, ponded lava over the vent drains back down into the magma chambers below. Open a beer can after shaking it. Beer sprays out because of the effervescing gas, and drains back into the can from the lid after the gas has escaped. The analogy is oversimplified but illustrates the principle.

39 Main vent at Kilauea Iki, spraying out a 300-meter-high fountain of lava. (Photograph by the U.S. Geological Survey, November 19, 1959.)

40 Ponded lava in Kilauea Iki crater forms a molten lake 100 meters deep. The level of the lava lake covers the main vent just prior to a period of drainback. (Photograph by the U.S. Geological Survey, December 5, 1959.)

41 Between periods of eruption, the upper few meters of Kilauea Iki lava lake drains back down into the main vent. During these periods of drainback, sections of the lava lake crust are pulled apart by the rapid flow, exposing the incandescent melt beneath along zig-zag lines. (Photograph by the U.S. Geological Survey, December 19, 1959.)

Some of the pumice and strands of volcanic glass called Pele's hair, which formed in the fire fountains, were blown downwind by the prevailing trade winds. This built a large cinder cone of lava fragments about 60 meters high on the south rim of Kilauea Iki crater (Figure 42).

The final lava lake in Kilauea Iki, 110 meters deep and about 1 kilometer in diameter, is still hot in 1980. The present crust is about 60 meters thick and covers a molten core about 5 meters thick.

After the end of the surface activity at Kilauea Iki on December 20, 1959, minor seismic tremor indicated that magma was still moving at depth. Tilt measurements indicated that renewed inflation was occurring and that the eruption was probably not over. A swarm of microearthquakes then began along the east rift of Kilauea about 40 kilometers from the summit, suggesting that magma inflating the summit region was also exerting pressure along the molten core of the rift zone. As the rift zone yielded, the microearthquakes revealed that fractures had begun to break toward the surface far down on the flank of Kilauea near sea level.

On January 13, earthquakes began to be felt near the village of Kapoho, 45 kilometers east of Kilauea's summit, and surface cracks started forming. Since an eruption seemed imminent, Kapoho was evacuated. At 7:30 PM lava started erupting from vents along a fissure over 1 kilometer long, and soon a dazzling curtain of fire fountains arose along the entire length of the fissure. Within two days the eruption concentrated to a main vent.

This process of an eruption beginning along a fissure and then localizing to a point-source vent is common in new eruption sites (Figure 43). The magma temperatures are high enough to melt some of the rock walls of the fracture. Where the fracture is by chance wider than average, more lava rushes out and more wall rock is melted. Any part of the fracture that was more open at the beginning of the eruption continues to become larger, thus robbing flow from the rest of the fracture.

Lava flow

Kilauea
Iki
crater

Halemaumau
crater

Keanakakoi
crater

42 Aerial view of Kilauea caldera before the Kilauea Iki eruption. Mauna Kea Volcano is
in the background. The caldera is 5 kilometers long (northeast–southwest) and 3 kilometers wide. Halemaumau crater at left-center is 1 kilometer in diameter. Kilauea Iki crater
is on the far right. (Photograph by the U.S. Geological Survey, November 1, 1954.)

43 After the Kilauea Iki eruption ceased, magma moved eastward beneath the east rift of Kilauea Volcano to the Kapoho area. Before the outbreak of lava there, this fault scarp broke the surface. (Photograph by the National Park Service, January 13, 1960.)

44 Leaves of these papaya trees were stripped by the falling pumice and cinder fragments from the main Kapoho eruption vent, seen in the background. (Photograph by the U.S. Geological Survey, January 16, 1960.)

The slower-flowing portions of the fracture begin to cool and seal themselves with solid rock, which in turn forces more of the erupting magma to the main vent.

During the early stages of the Kapoho eruption, steam and ash clouds as well as incandescent lava fountains were erupted from the fracture. Heated ground water flashing to steam was probably the cause of the more explosive emissions.

The main fountain, sometimes spraying to heights of 500 meters, soon produced a steady stream of lava which flowed through the lowlands and reached the sea by January 15. The flows covered Kapoho village, a Coast Guard station and a number of beach houses, but fortunately they moved so slowly that no lives were lost. By February 6, lava flows had ceased after covering 6 square kilometers of old Hawaii and forming 2

45 Lava from the Kapoho eruption enters the sea, forming 2 square kilometers of new land on Hawaii's eastern cape. (Photograph by the U.S. Geological Survey, January 15, 1960.)

square kilometers of new Hawaii in the sea (Figures 45 and 46). The Kapoho vent continued to erupt gas, pumice, and lava spatter for two more weeks, building a large cone 100 meters high.

The lava in the Kapoho eruption changed from an initial composition similar to that of a 1955 eruption on the east rift to a composition similar to that of the Kilauea Iki eruption, and the temperature of the lava increased from 1060°C to 1130°C. This suggests that some of the old magma stored in the core of the rift zone was erupted first and was then replaced by newer magma flowing along the rift zone core from the summit of Kilauea. Rapid subsidence of the summit of Kilauea in excess of one meter, as shown by the tiltmeters and re-leveling, took

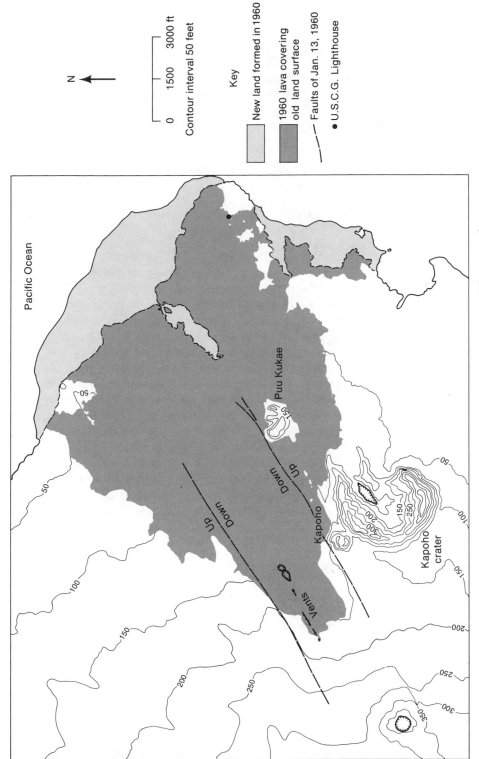

46 The 1960 flows at Kapoho, on the east rift of Kilauea, covered 6 square kilometers of old land surface and destroyed the village of Kapoho. Two new square kilometers of land formed beyond the old shoreline. (Map by the U.S. Geological Survey.)

place during the Kapoho eruption, confirming the source of the magma (Figure 47). The concept that magma can flow horizontally through the cores of the rift zones in the flanks of Hawaiian volcanoes was one of the major discoveries of the Kilauea Iki-Kapoho eruptions. The extensive use of seismographs and tiltmeters to track the subsurface activity of the volcano before and after the actual surface eruptions was also a major technical advance toward understanding the complex processes of volcanic activity. Pele, Hawaiian goddess of Earth and fire, is still quite unpredictable, but now she is a little less invisible.

Twenty-three eruptions on the summit and flanks of Kilauea have occurred between 1959 and 1980. The total volume of lava produced by these eruptions is about 0.8 cubic kilometer. Compare this with the 1.1 cubic kilometers erupted by Surtsey, mainly during its first year, and the 18 cubic kilometers erupted by Krakatau in one day. Such powers of nature are on a scale barely comprehensible even in a nuclear age.

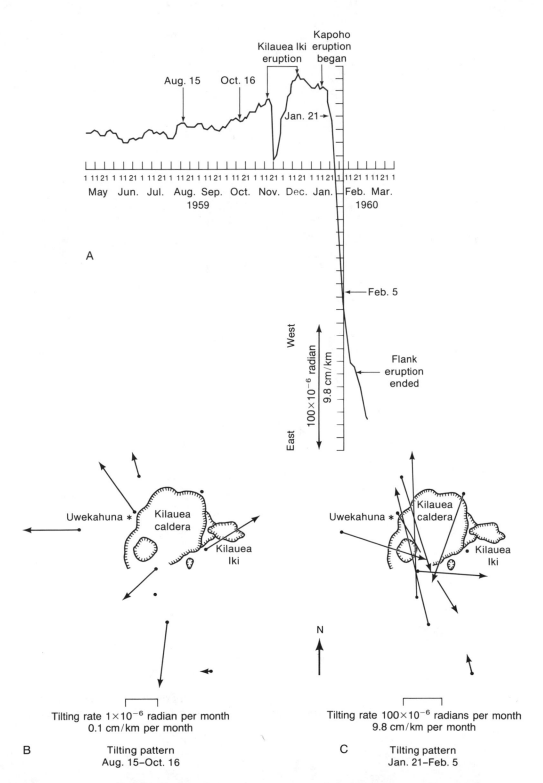

A

Aug. 15

Oct. 16

Kilauea Iki eruption

Kapoho eruption began

Jan. 21→

1 11 21 1 11 21 1 11 21 1 11 21 1 11 21 1 11 21 1 11 21 1 11 21 1 11 21 | 1 11 21 1 11 21 1

May Jun. Jul. Aug. Sep. Oct. Nov. Dec. Jan. Feb. Mar.

1959   1960

West

East

100×10^{-6} radian

9.8 cm/km

Feb. 5

Flank eruption ended

Uwekahuna *

Kilauea caldera

Kilauea Iki

Tilting rate 1×10^{-6} radian per month
0.1 cm/km per month

B   Tilting pattern
Aug. 15–Oct. 16

N

Uwekahuna *

Kilauea caldera

Kilauea Iki

Tilting rate 100×10^{-6} radians per month
9.8 cm/km per month

C   Tilting pattern
Jan. 21–Feb. 5

7

Hot Spots

7 Hot Spots

Stones rot. Only the chants remain.
Polynesian saying

The close connection between the edges of the moving plates of the Earth's crust and volcanoes has been emphasized in earlier chapters. Why then is the Island of Hawaii, with two of the world's most active volcanoes, located right in the middle of the Pacific plate (Figure 48)? Only 5 percent of the world's active volcanoes are located within plates, but even so there must be some reason for their existence.

There are some obvious differences between the Hawaiian volcanoes, which form a linear belt or chain, and volcanoes located on plate margins. Topography is one. A profile section of the Hawaiian Islands chain is completely different from a cross section of a spreading ridge or a subduction zone (Figure 49).

Another major difference is the age distribution of Hawaiian volcanoes compared to that of plate margin volcanoes. Geologists have recognized for over a hundred years that the islands in the Hawaiian chain become older as you move from the southeast to the northwest. Recorded eruptions have occurred only on Hawaii, at the southeast end of the chain; the islands to the northwest are lower and more eroded. The chain extends to Midway Island, 2500 kilometers northwest of the Big Island of Hawaii, where only a coral atoll cap covering a submerged volcanic peak marks the largely submarine ridge. The ages of the volcanic rocks of the Hawaiian Islands, obtained by radioactive

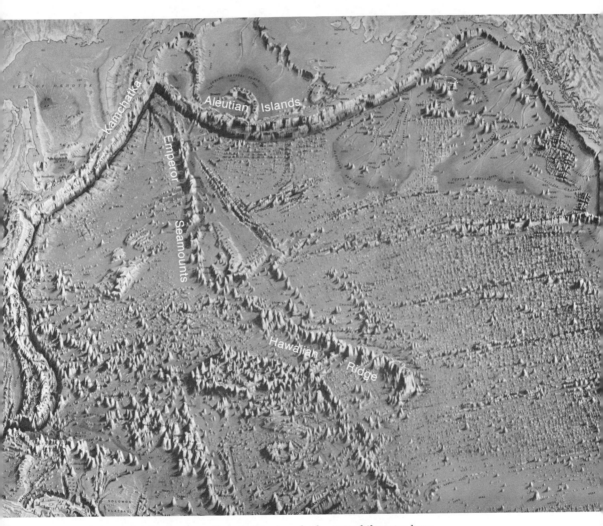

48 Hawaiian Islands rise from the southeast end of a 8000-kilometer-long dogleg chain of seamounts. The portion north of the bend is called the Emperor Seamounts; that south of the bend is called the Hawaiian Ridge. (Map from *World Ocean Floor Panorama* by Bruce C. Heezen and Marie Tharp, initiated and supported by the Office of Naval Research. Copyright Marie Tharp, 1977. Reproduced by permission of Marie Tharp, all rights reserved.)

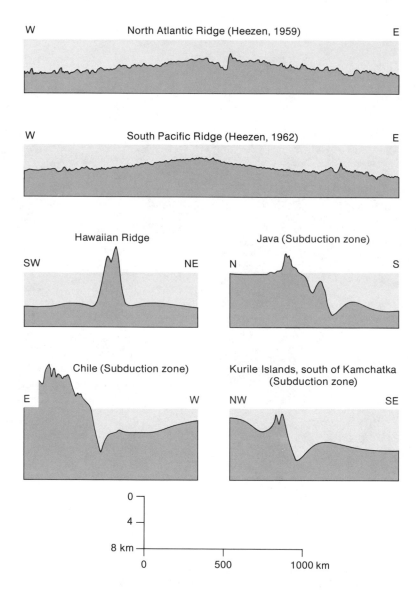

49 Comparison of topographic profiles of subduction zones, mid-ocean ridges, and Hawaii. Vertical scale is exaggerated 40 times. Island arcs and compressional mountains are basically asymmetrical, whereas mid-ocean ridges and Hawaii are symmetrical about a central axis. The width of the mid-ocean ridges is caused by sea-floor spreading.

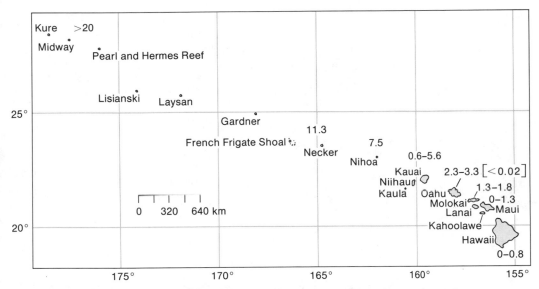

50 Ages of islands in the Hawaiian chain in millions of years. Islands get progressively older to the northwest. The apparent rate of movement away from the Hawaiian hot spot (deep source of magma), is 10 centimeters per year. The younger rock age shown in brackets applies to only a small volume from later eruptions that cannot be explained by the hot spot idea. (Data from Ian McDougall, *Bulletin of the Geological Society of America*, 75, 1964, p. 107; and G.A. Macdonald and A.T. Abbott, *Volcanoes in the Sea*, University of Hawaii Press, 1970.)

dating, confirm this picture. Rocks on the Big Island are all less than 1 million years old; most of the rocks on Oahu, the location of Honolulu and Pearl Harbor, are 2 to 3 million years old; and the ancient lava flows on Kauai, northwest of Oahu, are as much as 5 million years old (Figure 50).

This pattern of age distribution of Hawaiian volcanic rock is strikingly different from that of plate margin volcanoes. In subduction zones and on the oceanic ridges, the young volcanoes form a line along the seam of the plates; and on the oceanic ridges there is a progressive aging of the volcanic rocks on either side of the active belt. The Hawaiian chain is just the opposite; the volcanoes get older along the crest of the chain, instead of across the crest of the volcanic belt.

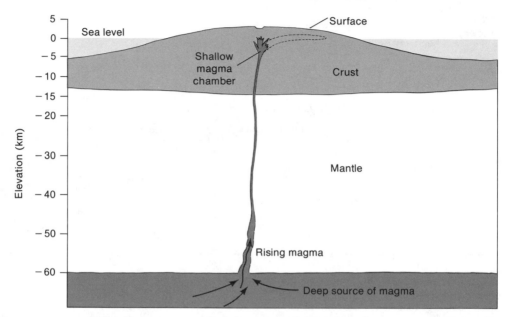

51 Schematic cross section of an active Hawaiian volcano. The vertical scale is exaggerated two times. The dotted line extending to the right from the shallow magma chamber is an inferred zone of feeder dikes to a rift zone. The deep source of magma, below 50 to 60 kilometers, and the shallow storage zone at 3 to 6 kilometers beneath the surface are the vital parts of the active system. (After Jerry Eaton, U.S. Geological Survey.)

Earthquakes, those close companions of active volcanoes, also show an unusual pattern in Hawaii. Earthquakes occur along the entire length of subduction zones and oceanic ridges, but in Hawaii they are common only at the southeast end of the chain, mostly beneath the Big Island.

The data from over 30,000 microearthquakes occurring near Kilauea Volcano on Hawaii, and the pattern of tilting that indicates swelling and contraction of a shallow reservoir of molten rock (a magma chamber) suggest an interesting subsurface model of a Hawaiian volcano (Figure 51).

Charting the location of the earthquakes at depth outlines the conduits through which the molten rock forces its way upward.

The propelling force is the buoyancy of the lighter molten rock surrounded by more dense crystalline rocks. As the magma rises, the hard surrounding rocks are cracked open by changing pressures and temperatures, causing earthquakes.

The deep source of magma appears to be within the plastic layer 50 to 60 kilometers beneath the Pacific plate, the maximum depth of the earthquakes. Graphs of the locations of the intermediate-to-deep earthquakes, 10 to 60 kilometers beneath Kilauea, over a period of years outline a vague vertical conduit a few kilometers in diameter and 50 kilometers high which allows the deep magma to come up into a shallow magma chamber 3 to 6 kilometers beneath the summit. This shallow chamber is bounded by a region of many microearthquakes, but has almost no earthquakes inside of it. Most earthquakes are thought to originate from the cracking and slipping of brittle rocks that suddenly fail by fracture. Plastic or liquid rock in a magma chamber can deform without breaking and thus doesn't cause earthquakes.

The tilt pattern near the summit of Kilauea supports this magma chamber model. Just as the pattern of tilting on the surface of an inflating balloon would indicate the radius of the balloon, the pattern of tilt at Kilauea indicates a pressure center about 4 kilometers deep. In this balloon analogy, the deep source of magma is the pump, the vertical conduit is the connecting hose, and the shallow magma chamber is the balloon (Figure 52).

The pattern of slow outward tilting or inflation of Kilauea prior to an eruption and the rapid inward tilting or deflation during a flank eruption indicates a slow, almost continuous movement of magma from the deep source to the shallow chamber, and rapid and intermittent eruptions from the shallow chamber to the surface. Because the rate of movement of magma from depth to the shallow chamber does not keep pace with the surface eruption rate, the eruption eventually stops until the shallow chamber is recharged.

But how does this relate to the origin and continuing vigor of the Hawaiian volcanic chain? There must be something unique about the location of the Island of Hawaii. Somehow deep magma must be more available at this location. Tuzo Wilson

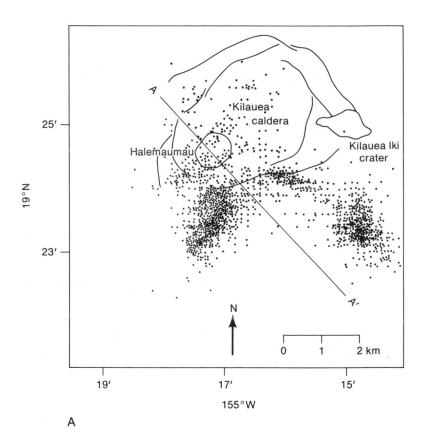

52 A. Map view of locations of shallow microearthquakes beneath Kilauea Volcano in Hawaii. Earthquakes are caused by rock fracture. Zones of no earthquakes are therefore regions of low stress or very low strength. Since high stresses prevail near most active volcanoes, the lack of earthquakes in a region surrounded by them suggests a plastic zone occupied by magma. The dense clusters of microearthquakes shown on the map indicate the beginning of the rift zones. B. *Opposite.* Cross-section of Kilauea caldera to a depth of 12 kilometers. (Data from Robert Koyanagi, U.S. Geological Survey.)

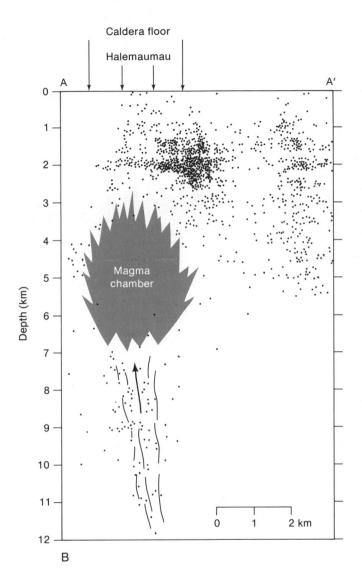

Caldera floor

Halemaumau

A   A'

Depth (km)

Magma chamber

0   1   2 km

B

suggested an elegantly simple explanation that fits neatly with the movement of the Pacific plate. He envisioned a hot plume of magma originating deep beneath the plate. This plume, or hot spot, stayed in the same location for millions of years as the plate slid over this source of magma. A volcano would grow over the hot spot and drift away with the slowly moving plate to be replaced by a new volcano growing over the same hot

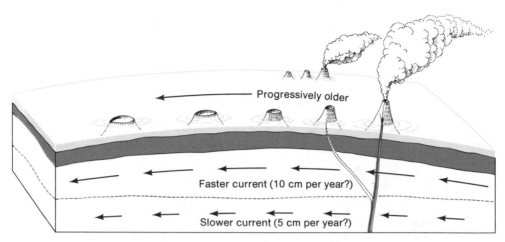

53 Original diagram used by Tuzo Wilson to suggest the origin of the Hawaiian Islands. The plate slowly moves over a relatively fixed source of magma, forming a new volcano as the older volcanoes are carried downstream. (From J. Tuzo Wilson, "Continental Drift." Copyright © 1963 by Scientific American, Inc. All rights reserved.)

spot, like smoke signals drifting in a gentle wind (Figure 53). Most geologists now accept the hot spot idea, but the concept is still more controversial than the larger scheme of plate tectonics.

The problem, of course, is in explaining the character of the hot spot. What keeps generating new magma at a relatively fixed spot within the Earth? The best theory now seems to be that the heat source of the hot spot is in the deep mantle, beneath the plastic layer. This implies that hot spot volcanoes may have even deeper ultimate sources for their magma than the volcanic belts along the plate margins (Figure 54).

If the hot spot theory is correct, the aging of volcanoes away from the hot spot should match the rate of plate movement. The magnetic stripe pattern on the ocean floor indicates the Pacific plate is moving northwest at about 10 to 12 centimeters per year. If Kauai has drifted northwest during the 5 million years since its lavas erupted, it should be 500 to 600 kilometers away from where it formed, which is the present location of the Big

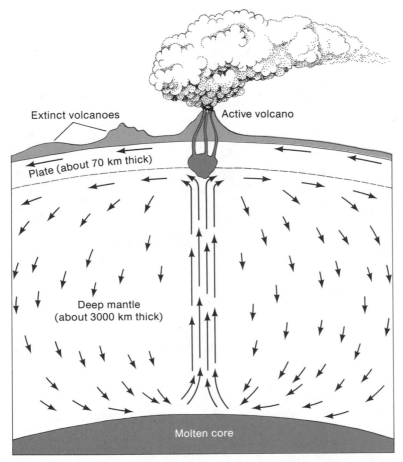

54 Deep mantle plumes generated by slow convection currents are one explanation of the relatively fixed position of hot spot volcanic sources. This concept, originated by Jason Morgan, is illustrated here. (After G.B. Dalrymple, E.A. Silver, and E.D. Jackson, "Origin of the Hawaiian Islands," *American Scientist* 61, March 1973, p. 306.)

Island. The actual distance is 560 kilometers, a striking verification of Wilson's idea or an amazing coincidence, depending on your belief.

Beyond Midway Island, the Hawaiian chain is a submerged line of seamounts continuing northwest another 1500 kilometers. After that, it meets a submerged mountain chain, the Emperor Seamounts, which trend north–northwest another 4000 kilometers toward Kamchatka. The Emperor Seamounts are

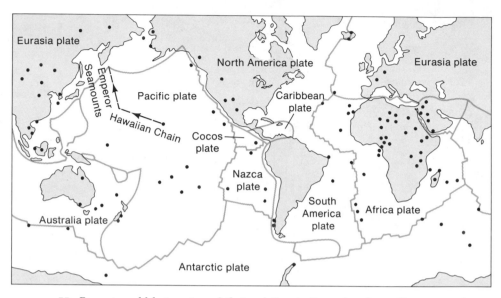

55 Present world hot spots and their relation to the major plates. Hot spot tracks, as illustrated by the Hawaii-Emperor trend, reveal past plate motions. Some geologists prefer a smaller number of hot spots. (After Kevin C. Burke and J. Tuzo Wilson, "Hot Spots on the Earth's Surface." Copyright © 1976 by Scientific American, Inc. All rights reserved.)

thought to be a dogleg of the Hawaiian chain formed when the drift of the Pacific plate was more northward than its present northwestward movement. The change in direction of plate movement, as estimated from the location of the bend, occurred about 40 million years ago. The great strength of the plate tectonics theory is that its predictions are substantiated by clues found in so many places around the world. The plates have left their tracks in the form of volcanic scars and magnetic fields, and those tracks yield a complex yet consistent global pattern.

At least two more seamount chains beneath the South Pacific indicate other major hot spots beneath the Pacific plate. Yellowstone Park, on the America plate, has been suggested as an active continental hot spot with the Snake River volcanic plain its earlier track. The Galapagos Islands on the equator off the west coast of South America is another group of very active volcanoes of probable hot spot origin (Figure 55).

The hot spot idea even offers a solution to the Iceland anomaly: the problem of why Iceland is the only part of the Mid-Atlantic ridge out of water. If Iceland is a hot spot that has become straddled by the ridge, then it has volcanoes of dual origin—both hot spot and oceanic ridge. This is an attractive explanation of the extra volcanism that has built Iceland above the sea.

No islands of similar origin could be more unlike than Hawaii and Iceland. Iceland is a rugged, nearly treeless land of harsh climate, inhabited by strong Vikings who have stalwartly maintained their culture and independence. Hawaii is a tropical garden, soft and seductive, inhabited by tourists who have almost submerged the Polynesian heritage. But both islands owe their distinct beauty, power, and mystery to their origins in volcanic fire.

8
Lava, Ash, and Bombs

8 Lava, Ash, and Bombs

A blast of burning sand pours out in whirling clouds.
Conspiring in their power, the rushing vapours
Carry up mountain blocks, black ash, and dazzling fire.
Lucilius Junior   (A.D. 50)

Volcanoes are dark windows to the interior of the Earth. Because their products are our only direct samples of the composition of the Earth's deeper levels, the aspect of volcanology analyzing those materials has received considerable study. Clues left behind in successive layers of volcanic rubble help describe the character and sequence of prehistoric eruptions, and provide a broader picture of volcanic events than historic activity can.

Most people think that lava flows are the only products spewed forth from volcanoes, but actually volcanic ash and larger solid fragments, called volcanic cinders and blocks, form the major products of observed volcanic eruptions. Lumping together all the sizes of solid fragments, geologists call this volcanic debris *pyroclastics*, which literally means fire fragments. Pyroclastics derive from three sources: magma that is cooled and broken into fragments by expanding gases at the moment of eruption; fragments of old crater walls which are ripped loose in explosive eruptions; and clots of liquid lava thrown into the air which cool during their flight.

Pyroclastic rocks are classified by the general size of the fragments. Volcanic dust is as fine as flour; volcanic ash is more gritty, with particles up to the size of rice; cinders include pieces as big as golf balls; and blocks cover everything up to chunks the size of a house. Volcanic bomb is a special term for block-sized clots of liquid lava thrown from erupting vents

56 A large volcanic bomb from Mauna Kea Volcano, Hawaii. This 50-kilogram specimen shows the twisted flow lines often acquired while these globs of hot plastic lava are spinning in flight. Pencil at bottom shows scale.

(Figure 56). The brilliant arcs on time-lapse photographs of volcanic eruptions are the traces of volcanic bombs in flight.

Pyroclastic rocks are erupted in two different ways: either as *airfall deposits* or as *pyroclastic flows*. Explosive volcanic eruptions often hurl fragments to great heights, and as the debris falls back to Earth it forms a distinct layer which blankets the slopes of the land. The falling process allows for some sorting of the debris; the coarser fragments fall first and nearby, while the dust is winnowed away to fall last, sometimes at

57 Volcanic ash layers in a road cut on Oshima Volcano, Japan. Airfall material is characterized by distinct layers which follow the slopes of the ground surface on which they fell. Two generations of ashfalls are seen here separated by an erosional surface. The beds are not folded; the inclined layers are the original attitude in which they accumulated.

great distances. Airfall deposits can be recognized by this layering and sorting (Figure 57).

Sometimes explosive volcanic eruptions produce a cloud of volcanic debris so charged with fragments that it is too heavy to rise. This emulsion of gas and fragments forms a glowing avalanche or nuée ardente, the most dangerous kind of volcanic hazard. Glowing avalanches travel up to 100 kilometers per hour, and flatten and burn most everything in their paths, as they did at Mont Pelée mentioned in Chapter 5. Small glowing avalanches often flow down the valleys on a volcano's flanks, but larger masses expelled at high speeds, or accelerated by steep slopes, can sweep over small hills or across large flat areas in their path. Glowing avalanche deposits pile up in low-lying areas after the avalanche loses its speed. These pyroclas-

58 Cast of a dead dog buried by volcanic ashes at Pompeii. During excavation, holes are found with skeletal remains inside. By carefully injecting the hole with plaster, a cast of the corpse is formed. About 2000 human victims have been unearthed at Pompeii. (Alinari/Editorial Photocolor Archives, Inc.)

tic flow deposits are distinct from airfall debris: they exhibit only vague layering and almost no sorting of the finer and coarser fragments. Roads cut in airfall deposits show a sharp banding of coarse and fine layers, often of different colors, while cuts in pyroclastic flows show massive deposits that look like pink or buff concrete.

The contrast in explosive debris around a volcano tells something of the nature of its previous eruptions and thus helps to predict the nature of possible future eruptions. For example, at Pompeii, the Roman city buried in volcanic ash from Vesuvius, the beginning of the 79 A.D. eruption produced several distinct layers of airfall deposits, but the upper layers of ash are more vague and have the character of pyroclastic flows. This would explain the relatively small number of bodies found buried at Pompeii; most people escaped during the early rain of ashes, but stragglers were smothered and buried by the later glowing avalanches (Figure 58).

Many subduction zone volcanoes have eruptions that begin with pyroclastic emissions and end with lava flows. This may be because there are higher concentrations of gas in the upper parts of magma chambers or because the shallow magma, erupted first, is cooler and more solid. No one is sure, for measurements of gas content and magma temperatures just prior to eruptions simply don't exist.

Oceanic ridge volcanoes and Hawaiian volcanoes erupt mainly lava flows. If we count the unseen flows deep beneath the sea, lava becomes the major product of all of the Earth's volcanoes. Shallow submarine eruptions like Surtsey can build an island of volcanic ash, but the great volume goes into streams of underwater lava.

Individual lava flows are tonguelike in shape, much longer than they are wide. On the Island of Hawaii a typical lava flow might be 10 kilometers long, 200 meters wide, and 3 meters thick; but there is so much variation that any standard flow dimensions can be misleading. Each eruption covers only a small fraction of the island with a finger of lava. This finger forms a low ridge, and later flows will either run beside the ridge or between ridges formed by earlier eruptions. The process is like covering a jug with candle drippings; it takes hundreds of wax flows to build up a covering layer. The volcanic pile above sea level on the Island of Hawaii is the accumulation of literally hundreds of thousands of lava flows.

A lava flow is hypnotic to watch. There is often a central river of orange-red molten rock 5 to 10 meters across, flowing at speeds of 5 to 50 kilometers per hour depending on the slope. The flow then oozes out on all sides from this central stream and forms slowly advancing dark lobes of cooling lava rubble riding on a molten but unseen core of the flow. These lava blocks tumble down the steep front of the advancing flow, giving a glimpse of the glowing interior, and are slowly overridden by the advancing flow. The growing edges and fronts of the flow look like giant slow-motion bulldozer treads moving out, down, and under as the mass of the flow spreads forward. The perimeter of the dark, growing flow is much larger than the central river of glowing, fast-flowing lava (Figure 59).

59 Flowing basalt lavas, especially aa, often have central channels that move at several kilometers per hour. These channels are red-hot (in this photograph light gray) in contrast to the partly cooled, black margins of the flow which advance more slowly, at rates of several meters per hour. (Photograph of the 1977 eruption of Piton de la Fournaise on Reunion Island by Pierre Vincent.)

In Hawaii, the kind of lava flow just described is called an *aa* flow, pronounced *aħ ah*. Its major characteristic is the rubble of broken lava blocks on its surface. Adventurers with thick boots have walked on these rubble surfaces while the flows are still slowly moving, but aa flows are hard enough on boots after they have stopped and cooled.

Another kind of Hawaiian lava flow is called *pahoehoe*, pronounced *pa ħóy hoy*. These flows are generally thinner than the aa flows and form a smooth to wrinkled surface of solid rock. Old Hawaiian foot trails favor the ancient pahoehoe flows and for good reason. Bare feet will last for many more kilometers on their smoother, more solid surfaces (Figure 60).

TABLE 1
Form of volcanic products

Form	*Name*	*Characteristics (dimensions)*
Gas	Fume	
	Lavas	
Liquid	Aa	rough, blocky surface
	Pahoehoe	smooth to ropy surface
	Airfall fragments	
Solid	dust	$< \frac{1}{16}$ mm
	ash	$\frac{1}{16}$–2 mm
	cinders	2–64 mm
	blocks	>64 mm solid
	bombs	>64 mm plastic
	Pyroclastic flows	hot fluidized flows
	Mudflows	flows fluidized by rainfall, melting ice and snow, or ejected crater lakes

60 Lava flows of aa (left) and pahoehoe both issued from Kilauea Volcano in Hawaii in 1974. The dark, rough aa is about 3 to 4 meters thick; it was covering the smoother, glistening pahoehoe when the flow stopped.

Sometimes lava rivers crust over and form tunnels filled with fast moving streams of lava. As an eruption wanes, the lava in these tunnels drains out, leaving empty caves known as lava tubes within the cooled flows. These tubes are 1 to 10 meters in diameter; some can be followed underground for hundreds of meters.

The barren smooth surfaces of pahoehoe flows compared to the rubble that forms aa flows are so distinctive that the Icelanders also have two separate words—*helluhraun* for pahoehoe and *apalhraun* for aa—to describe them where they occur in Iceland. The largest lava flow of historic record was an aa (apalhraun) flow that issued from a 25-kilometer-long fissure in Iceland in 1783. Called the Laki flow, it covered over 500 square kilometers with lava, completely filling two deep river valleys in the process. The volume of lava produced by the Laki fissure during several months of eruption was 12 cubic kilometers, enough to fill Yosemite Valley to a depth of 300 meters (Figure 61).

The texture of lava and volcanic ash is largely controlled by the number and size of gas bubble holes in the rock. Pumice is one extreme, being mostly holes. This frozen glass froth is so light that pieces of it float on water. Dense, solid rock without holes is the other extreme, and is less common than pumice. Most volcanic rocks are somewhere in between (Figure 62).

Magma is a melt of silicate compounds of variable composition. The common elements in the melt are oxygen, silicon, aluminum, iron, calcium, magnesium, sodium, titanium, and potassium. Silica, the compound of one silicon and two oxygen atoms (SiO_2) is the most abundant constituent; alumina (Al_2O_3) is second. The proportion of silica varies from about 45 to 70 percent of the total. Various types of magma and their resultant igneous rocks are classified by their silica content.

Geologists love to give fancy names to rocks, and there are hundreds of varieties. However, most volcanic rocks fall into one of three clans: basalt, andesite, or rhyolite, which have a silica content of about 50 percent, 60 percent, and 70 percent.

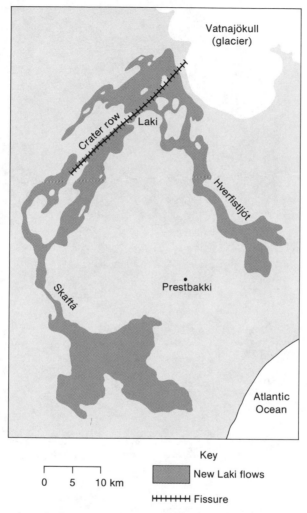

Key

New Laki flows

├┼┼┼┼┼┤ Fissure

0   5   10 km

61 Laki flow in South Central Iceland. The 1783 eruption
from a 25-kilometer-long fissure produced 565 square kilometers (12 cubic kilometers) of basaltic lava flows, a world
record. (Map data from Sigurdur Thorarinsson.)

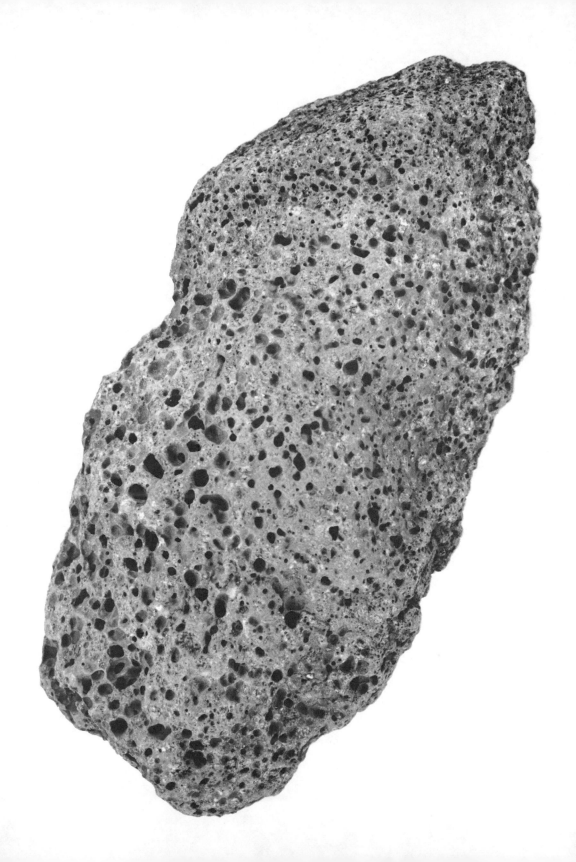

62 *Opposite.* Basaltic lava is often filled with gas bubble holes formed when steam and other gases dissolved in the magma are released by the low pressures at the Earth's surface. Tops of flows usually have more trapped bubble holes (vesicles) than the centers of flows. The small crystals are olivine, one of the first minerals to form from the cooling melt. (Photograph at true scale by James Griggs, U.S. Geological Survey.)

Rocks that contain more silica also contain more sodium and potassium and less iron, calcium, and magnesium. These last three elements, particularly the iron, form dark minerals, so that basalts are dark gray, almost black; andesites are medium gray; and rhyolites are light gray to light brown. One important exception is obsidian, a glassy form of rhyolite often used for arrowheads. Obsidian is nearly black. Although there is less iron in rhyolite, in obsidian it is so finely divided into tiny crystals of opaque iron oxides that it makes the glass look shiny black.

The chemistry of volcanic rocks is only part of the story of their complex composition. As magma cools, various minerals start to crystallize from the melt. Crystallization takes time. If the magma cools rapidly, within seconds or minutes, the compounds do not have time to arrange themselves into minerals, and the result is a dark, opaque glass. If the magma cools more slowly, within days or years, the minerals have time to form and grow.

The cooling of molten basalt in Kilauea Iki lava lake is a good example of volcanic rock formation. The lava was erupted at temperatures up to 1200 °C, and was nearly all liquid except for a few percent of small olivine crystals. Most of the water and other gases dissolved in the magma were vaporized and lost in the fume from the fire fountains, as the lava welled out of the vent and ponded in the older crater. The surface of the lake cooled quickly and formed a glassy crust with many bubble holes. The deeper crust formed more slowly because of the insulating effect of the overlying crust, and crystals of various minerals began to appear. Since olivine crystallized first, at temperatures from 1250 to 1190°C, some crystals were present at the time of eruption. Pyroxene formed next at temperatures between 1190 and 1180°C, and then plagioclase feldspar at 1170 to 1160°C. By the time the temperature had dropped to 1065°C the basalt was half liquid and half crystals of plagioclase, pyroxene, and olivine, and had become hard enough so that steel probes could not be pushed into this mixture at the bottom of shallow drill holes. Magnetite began to crystallize at 1030°C, forming black mineral grains that give the basalt much of its dark color. By 980°C the basalt was all crystals except for 5 to 10 percent glass. It was still red hot, but had effectively become a solid.

During cooling and crystallization, the composition of each mineral is quite different from the overall composition of the original magma. This differentiation keeps changing the composition of the remaining melt fraction as crystallization becomes more complete (Figure 63). The most evident effect is in the composition of the final interstitial glass by the time cooling has reached 980°C. That glass has a silica content of 60 percent, compared to 48 percent in the original melt.

The cooling of andesite and rhyolite magma is equally complex, and other silicate minerals including quartz become important constituents of their crystallization into volcanic rocks. The important difference between rocks formed from a cooling silicate magma and ice formed by cooling water is the mixture of minerals in igneous rocks. Water freezes at 0°C and forms only one mineral; magma freezes from 1250°C down to 700°C and there are two or three, or more, minerals in the final solid rock.

The volumes of lava and pyroclastic rocks produced in individual historic eruptions range from a few cubic meters up to 20 cubic kilometers. On the average, subduction zone volcanoes produce about 1 cubic kilometer of new volcanic rock each year, composed mostly of pyroclastics.

The volume of volcanic rocks produced by the oceanic ridge volcanoes is largely hidden in the deep oceans, but it can be estimated indirectly. The spreading rates and sizes of the plates

63 Photomicrograph of a very thin slice of Hawaiian basalt from Kilauea Iki lava lake. Drilling core-holes into the slowly cooling lake provides samples of "quick-frozen" basalt in which the drilling water suddenly chills the slowly cooling melt and arrests the process of crystallization. The uniform gray area surrounding the silicate crystals is glass formed from the sudden cooling of the melt. (Photograph by the U.S. Geological Survey.)

are reasonably well established and these data allow an estimate of the new area of seafloor that must be created every year to fill in the opening cracks between the spreading plates; the figure is about 2.5 square kilometers per year. Allowing 1 kilometer for the average thickness of the basalt flows that form the seafloor, the average amount of oceanic ridge volcanic products is about 2.5 cubic kilometers per year.

Hawaiian volcanoes average about 0.1 cubic kilometer per year of basalt lava flows, but the total for all hot-spot volcanoes is difficult to estimate because of the long intervals between eruptions in places like Yellowstone. A reasonable guess is an average of 0.5 cubic kilometer per year for the volcanic products of hot spots. The Earth's present volcanoes thus have a total output of about 4 cubic kilometers of new rock each year on the average. Many years go by without large volcanic eruptions, and then a Krakatau-type eruption comes along to catch up on the lag.

Huge deposits of pyroclastic flows that cover thousands of square kilometers and are tens to hundreds of meters thick exist in Japan, New Zealand, Central America, the western United States, and many other volcanic regions of the world. Some of these deposits give every indication that they were poured out in a single enormous eruption that would dwarf Krakatau. The volume in these deposits is on the order of 100 to 1000 cubic kilometers compared to the 18 cubic kilometers of Krakatau. This raises some fundamental questions. Was prehistoric volcanism, say a million years ago, greater than it is now? Or is the time span of recorded volcanic eruptions so short, about two hundred years, that the data we have cover too short a time to be representative? We think the latter is true. Krakatau is probably only a small sample of what nature can deliver in the way of a volcanic cataclysm.

Opposite. El Cotopaxi, Ecuador.
(Photograph by G.E. Lewis, U.S. Geological Survey.)

9
Cones and Craters

9 Cones and Craters

*Only to a magician is the world forever fluid, infinitely
mutable and eternally new. Only he knows the secret
of change, only he knows truly that all things are
crouched in eagerness to become something else, and it is
from this universal tension that he draws his power.*
Peter Beagle   (1976)

Mountains come in different styles. Some, like the Himalayas,
form where the crust of the continents is telescoped together by
powerful compressive forces. Others, like the ranges between
the Rockies and the Sierra Nevada, form by the down faulting
of keystone blocks as the crust pulls apart under tension. Still
others, such as the Appalachians, result from regional uplift
and the subsequent etching by erosion of hard and soft rock
formations—folded by earlier compression—to form ridges
and valleys.

Volcanoes are a mountain style all their own. They are built
upon the landscape by outpourings of new rock. Their forms
change rapidly, some even during a person's lifetime. In the
Tolbachik region of Kamchatka, a new cinder cone grew to a
height of 600 meters in just four months in 1975.

Geologists learn that the hills are not everlasting, that erosion
slowly strips away the mountains and fills the intervening basins with their debris. It is usually taken for granted these days
that river valleys were carved out by the streams they contain.
But move to an active volcanic terrain and all the rules change.
The mountains are growing, new rocks are forming, and the
valleys are often the spaces between lava flows. In other words,
some valleys were not formed by erosion, but by lack of con-
struction. Even experienced geologists must remind themselves that they are in a strange land where the rules are often
reversed.

64 Summit of Cotopaxi Volcano, Ecuador. The nested craters result from explosive erup- tions of different intensities. Snow and ice dominate the summit of this 5900-meter peak despite its volcanic activity and its location less than one degree south of the equator. (Photograph by G.E. Lewis, U.S. Geological Survey.)

Volcanoes form some of the most beautiful and unusual land- scapes on Earth. Their power and fire command respect and remind one of the intense vitality of our Earth. *Kazan*, the Japa- nese word for volcano, means fire mountain; our word volcano is the name of an island near Italy whose volcanic peak was considered the forge of Vulcan, the Roman god of weapons.

Volcanic mountains have shapes that range from the perfect cones of Mount Fuji in Japan and Mayon in the Philippines, to flat lava plateaus in Iceland that barely meet the designation of mountain. Their craters range from vast circular basins called calderas, several kilometers in diameter, to tiny vents a few meters across. Several factors are at work in producing these great variations in form.

The shape of the vent from which the volcanic products escape to the surface is of prime importance. It is usually a long, nearly vertical crack in the ground, several hundreds to thousands of meters long and deep, and only a few meters wide. Magma rises through this fracture and issues along a linear vent at the surface. The Laki eruption in Iceland and the beginning of the Kilauea Iki eruption in Hawaii are examples of eruptions from linear vents.

A specific location along a linear vent often becomes the major source of volcanic emissions as an eruption progresses, forming a central vent from which a volcanic mountain begins to grow. If a volcano is eroded down to its roots, the chilled magma in the exposed feeding cracks is seen as long low ridges with greater resistance to erosion. These features are called volcanic dikes. The eroded remnant of a steep pipelike conduit which feeds a central vent is called a volcanic neck (Figure 65).

The viscosity of the magma as it erupts also has a profound impact on the shape of volcanoes. Very viscous lavas form a steep-sided plug over the vent called a lava dome. Solid fragments thrown from a vent form a pile of debris around or downwind from the crater called a cinder cone. Debris cones have very straight sides with slopes of about 30°, the angle of repose above which the cinders will slide until the stable angle is established. Very fluid lavas, on the other hand, flow long distances on gentle slopes, forming lava plateaus or low-sloping volcanic piles called shield volcanoes. Since the composition of a lava is generally related to its viscosity—basalt is more fluid and rhyolite more viscous—the shape of a volcano is often an important clue to its composition.

Many explosive volcanoes begin an eruption with volcanic ash followed by lava flows. The alternation of ash and flows forms the steep concave slopes of the classic volcanic cone. The scientific name for this type of structure is strato-volcano, or composite cone, because of the layering of volcanic ash and lava flows (Figures 66, 67, and 68).

The surface environment of the volcanic vent also has a major effect on the shape of the resulting volcano. Submarine

65 Ship Rock in New Mexico is a volcanic neck with radiating dikes. Erosion has stripped away the volcanic cone, leaving only the hard skeletal remains. Ship Rock is 450 meters high and the dikes form great walls stretching across the desert. (Photograph from *Geology Illustrated*, by John S. Shelton, p. 15. W.H. Freeman and Company. Copyright ©️ 1966.]

volcanoes are the best examples of the effects of environmental factors. As explained in Chapter 3, deep submarine volcanoes are not explosive because the water pressure is so great that steam cannot form and expand. However, the water chills the lava faster than the air would, so the lava piles are more steep-sided than those same lavas would be if they were erupted above water. Shallow submarine eruptions are usually explosive, even when they involve basalt magma that would be poured out in relatively quiet fountains and flows on land.

Volcanic eruptions beneath thick piles of glacial ice show many of the same features as submarine eruptions: deep outpourings of pillow lavas, followed by shallow-water explosions of volcanic debris, and capped by gently sloping flows of lava that reached above the glacial surface. The table mountain vol-

66 *Opposite.* Mayon Volcano, Philippines, in eruption. The rising ash column and descending nuée ardente partly conceal the perfect symmetry of Mayon's strato-volcano cone. (Photograph by Dainty Studio, Daraga, Albay, Philippines, April 30, 1968.)

67 Initial stages of an explosion cloud forming on Lassen Peak in California. This strato-volcano with a summit lava dome erupted from 1914 to 1917. (Photograph by B.F. Loomis, June 14, 1914, courtesy of the National Park Service.)

68 Santiago Crater of Masaya Volcano in Nicaragua reveals the inner structure of a strato-volcano. The light layers are lava flows and the dark layers are ash falls. The thick dark layer at the top is part of a cinder cone whose summit is just to the left of this photograph.

69 Herdubreid, a table mountain in Iceland. Pillow lavas on the steep flanks covered by gently sloping flows on the summit indicate that table mountains were formed by eruptions beneath a glacial ice cap. The elevation to the edge of the table marks the thickness of the ice. (Photograph by Gudmundur Sigvaldason.)

canoes of Iceland are thought to have originated in this way (Figure 69). The glacial ice caps are now largely gone, but the steep shoulders on the table mountains mark their former thickness.

Other factors such as the volume of erupted material and the length of time between eruptions also influence the form of a volcano. Small volumes of pyroclastic flows fill valleys, while huge pyroclastic flows form plateaus that bury all the underlying topography. Los Alamos, New Mexico, is located on a volcanic plateau formed 1.5 million years ago (Figure 70). Plateaus of pyroclastic flow material are common in many volcanic regions of the world. Fortunately, none have formed in historic time. Their great size and speed of emplacement would be cataclysmic.

The craters on volcanoes are also formed in many ways. Funnel-shaped craters usually result from an initial enlargement of the vent by volcanic explosions followed by the collapse of loose debris back into the crater at the end of the eruption. After

70 Los Alamos, New Mexico, the birthplace of nuclear power, lies on the flank of a giant prehistoric volcano. The city sprawls across a canyon-cut plateau of thick ash flow deposits, erupted about 1 million years ago. Ejection of this huge volume of ash caused the volcanic summit to collapse forming Valle Grande, the 20-kilometer-diameter caldera covered by grasslands in the background. (Photograph by William Regan of the Los Alamos Scientific Laboratory.)

gas escapes from magma, the reduction in volume sometimes allows the magma to drain back down the vent, forming a deep cylindrical crater on the volcano's summit. The crater on Mount Fuji is about 700 meters in diameter and 100 meters deep with nearly vertical walls.

Craters are sometimes filled with domes of viscous lava, and the rows of small craters along an erupting fissure can be buried by the thick lava flows that issue from them. The lack of cones and craters on extensive lava plateaus such as the Columbia River lava fields in Washington and Oregon make it difficult to locate the actual vents from which the lavas erupted.

When a volcano erupts a very large volume of magma, the void created underground cannot support itself and part of the volcano subsides, or collapses, into the emptied space. The collapse creates a large circular basin with steep walls, sometimes several hundred meters high; many such basins are the remains of the summit of an earlier volcanic cone. Collapse calderas form within a few hours or days, as at Krakatau, and are generally associated with great eruptions. The caldera at Valle Grande, just west of Los Alamos, is 16 kilometers in diameter and about 1 kilometer deep. It apparently resulted from the sudden collapse associated with the 300 cubic kilometers of ash flows that violently erupted and formed the pyroclastic plateaus that surround the caldera. Crater Lake in Oregon is another collapse caldera. It formed during a great eruption that occurred about 6000 years ago, as dated by the carbon 14 in the trees incinerated to charcoal beneath the pyroclastic flows.

Calderas also form on the nonexplosive Hawaiian volcanoes. The summits of the major shield volcanoes Mauna Loa and Kilauea have large elliptical calderas 3 to 5 kilometers in diameter with vertical walls up to 200 meters high (Figure 71). These calderas formed in prehistoric times, but the absence of explosive volcanic debris around their rims indicates that they formed by the collapse associated with the removal of considerable magma from the summit chambers. Large flank eruptions of lava are thought to have caused the magma removal and caldera collapse.

71 Circular craters and a large 3-by-5-kilometer caldera indent the snow-covered summit of Mauna Loa Volcano in Hawaii. These collapse features with cliffs up to 200 meters high lie at an elevation of about 4000 meters, at the top of a huge gently sloping shield volcano. Historic eruptions have been filling the craters and caldera with numerous flows. (Photograph by the U.S. Army Airforce in 1939; courtesy of the National Archives.)

Craters and calderas are difficult to tell apart, and in fact Kilauea caldera is often called Kilauea crater, even on official maps. A practical though arbitrary distinction can be made on the basis of size. Craters are smaller than 1 kilometer in diameter; calderas are larger than 1 kilometer in diameter.

Volcanic mountains evolve through time; their mature and old-age forms are far from simple. A cinder cone is often the early stage of a strato-volcano. Caldera collapse may then swallow up the summit of a large strato-volcano, and new lava domes may subsequently appear over several vents along the rim of the caldera. One way out of this classification dilemma is to call the result a complex volcano, or volcanic complex. Even so, with careful geologic mapping it is often possible to distinguish the component parts of a volcanic complex and the order in which they formed. The history of eruptive habits and their sequence can be very useful in attempting to forecast the future hazards at a particular volcano (Figure 72).

Volcanoes can be erupting, dormant, or dead. Their lifetimes are extremely variable. The great volcanic complex of the Valle Grande has been erupting intermittently for 15 million years. Most individual volcanoes in Iceland erupt only once, suggesting that Surtsey's lifetime was only 5 years. An average life span for a recurrently erupting volcano is roughly a million years. In the end, erosion takes over and the stumps of vanquished volcanoes join the other passive mountains of the world.

The time of death can be estimated from the degree of erosion, but such estimates must be made with caution. Erosion itself is extremely variable; fast in wet, humid climates, slower in cold, dry regions. In Hawaii there are vast climatic changes over short distances. The low slopes facing the trade winds are hot and humid and sustain more than 5 meters of rainfall per year. On the summit of Mauna Loa it is cold and relatively dry, and on the lee shore of Hawaii the climate is that of a desert. Lava flows only 50 years old have been reclaimed to soil and jungle in the hot humid areas, while flows 1000 years old high on Mauna Loa look freshly erupted. In the high deserts of Mexico, cinder cones remain almost untouched by erosion for thousands of years.

But climates change and the tooth of time finally wears down all volcanoes. Since its formation 1.5 million years ago, half of the Los Alamos plateau has been incised by deep canyons. Islands like Hawaii are washed completely away by the sea in 5 to 10 million years, and then slowly subside beneath a growing coral atoll cap.

We have records of volcanic activity for 2000 years in Europe, 1000 years in Iceland, and only a little over 100 years in the northwestern United States. Comparing this with a million-year volcanic life span and a similar time to erode away the dead cones and craters, it is folly to declare a volcano extinct just because it has had no historic eruptions. Any volcanic peak that shows little of the ravages of time, such as Mount Rainier, Mount Hood, or Mount Shasta, is only dormant (Figure 73).

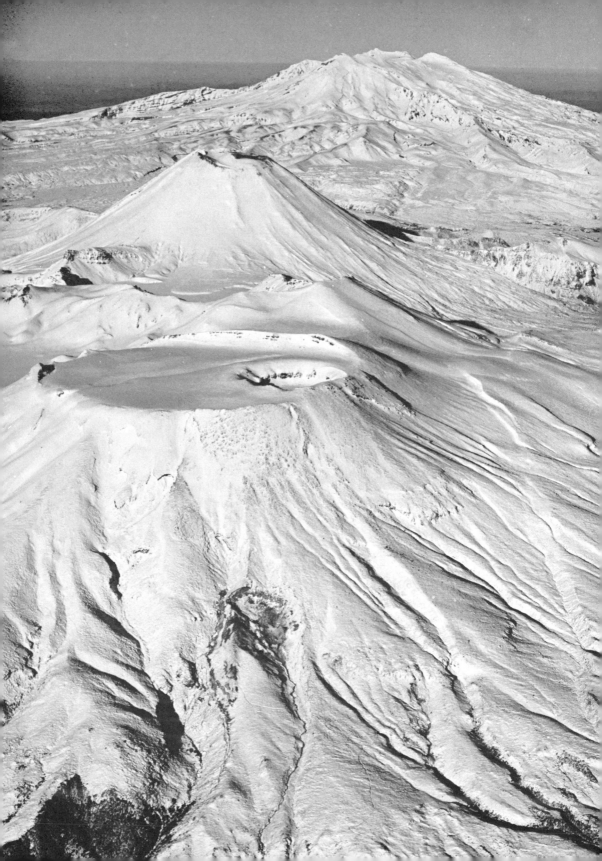

72 *Opposite.* Aerial view of Tongariro, Ngauruhoe, and Ruapehu volcanoes in New Zealand. The crater of Tongariro, in the foreground, is 1.3 kilometers wide and is transitional between a large crater and a small caldera. It is filled by ponded prehistoric flows cut by a small collapse crater. The cone of Ngauruhoe, in the middleground, is typical of an active strato-volcano with a summit crater. Ruapehu, in the background, is also an active strato-volcano, but it contains a crater lake whose eruptions have prematurely eroded the volcano's flanks. (Photograph by S.N. Beatus, New Zealand Geological Survey.)

73 Mount Rainier, a massive strato-volcano in the Cascade Range of Washington. Several valley glaciers fed by heavy snowfalls have begun to erode this 4392-meter active volcano. (Photograph by Norman Bishop, National Park Service.)

10

Roots of Volcanoes

10 Roots of Volcanoes

Men argue, Nature acts.
Voltaire (1694–1778)

When John Wesley Powell was trying to establish the U.S. Geological Survey, the Senator from Nebraska challenged Powell by saying "You can't see any farther into the Earth than any other man." Even today geologists can hardly deny the truth of this statement, but we do have a great deal of indirect data on the inside of the Earth which helps to guide our speculations.

For example, we can study the seismic waves from large earthquakes because they travel through the Earth to seismograph stations around the entire globe. Earthquake waves change in character as they travel away from their source; but regardless of the location of the earthquake, seismographic recordings made at equal distances from the source are remarkably the same. This result can only be explained by an interior structure of the Earth that is symmetrical about the center (Figure 74). Thus if the Earth's interior is composed of various materials, they must be arranged in layers or spherical shells like an onion.

We also have clues to the weight of the Earth's interior. We know the average density of the whole Earth from the magnitude of the force of gravity at the Earth's surface; it amounts to 5.5 grams per cubic centimeter, which is twice the density of surface rocks. Therefore, some parts of the Earth's interior must be very dense material to bring the average up to 5.5.

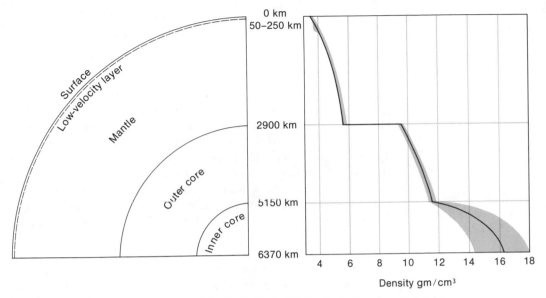

74 Estimated density of the interior of the Earth. The solid line in the graph on the right shows the most probable value of density at each depth, and the shaded region outlines the range of uncertainty. (Data from K.E. Bullen, "The Interior of the Earth." Copyright © 1955, Scientific American, Inc. All rights reserved.)

Reasonable speculations on the roots of volcanoes must be consistent with our knowledge of the physics and chemistry of the whole Earth as well as with our observations on the surface geology. One fact is quite clear: the surface geology indicates that our Earth is very complex and heterogeneous. However, the physical and chemical data on the Earth's interior yield average values rather than details, so most models of the Earth's interior show simple shells of rock or molten metals of homogeneous composition. As a first approximation these cartoons are probably right, but the details are missing. Filling in this picture is the most fascinating challenge in geoscience research today.

These details are not trivial. Diamond and graphite are the same chemical, but wars have been fought over their difference. Synthetic diamonds can be made from graphite with complex high-pressure, high-temperature furnaces reaching ranges of 100,000 atmospheres at over 1000°C. Natural diamonds occur in volcanic pipes that have originated at depths of up to 200 kilometers beneath the surface; thus the diamonds, their inclusions, and the pieces of wall rock erupted with them provide a direct sample of the composition, pressure, and temperature at depths in the Earth far below the reach of drilling.

The uplift and erosion of ancient volcanoes expose their shallow roots that were once as much as 10 kilometers below the surface. Post mortems on these rocks show that the dikes and pipes of chilled magma often connected surface vents to larger storage chambers of molten rock at depths of 2 to 10 kilometers beneath the surface. These shallow magma chambers were complex bodies of intersecting dikes and layers of molten rock, or sometimes more cylindrical masses called stocks or plutons. Their composition, the texture of their crystals, and the host rocks at their edges yield important clues to how the magma chambers were emplaced, and how and when they cooled into crystalline rocks. In general, the composition of shallow magma chambers is the same as that of surface volcanic products, but their texture is more coarsely crystalline because they cooled more slowly. For example, granite is the root rock in stocks beneath volcanoes that once erupted rhyolite lava flows or huge volumes of rhyolitic pyroclastic flows (Table 2).

TABLE 2
Types of igneous rock

	Extrusive (erupted on surface)	Intrusive (solidified below surface)
About 50% SiO_2	basalt	gabbro
About 60% SiO_2	andesite	diorite
About 70% SiO_2	rhyolite	granite

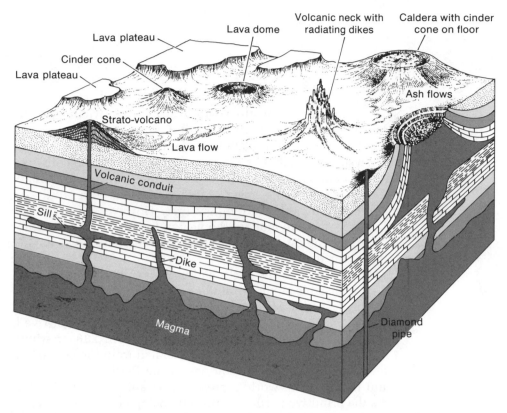

75 Schematic diagram of the surface forms and subsurface structure of various volcanic features. (After R.G. Schmidt and H.R. Shaw, *Atlas of Volcanic Phenomena,* U.S. Geological Survey, 1972.)

However, shallow magma chambers are not the deep roots of volcanoes. They occur at depths too shallow for rocks to be melted by the Earth's heat. Uplift and erosion have not exposed the deep roots of volcanoes; they are still hidden from direct observation so our information about them is more tenuous. The sources of the heat that melts rocks are still under lively debate. The leading contenders include the Earth's original heat from the time of formation; heat from the breakdown of the radioactive isotopes of uranium, thorium, and potassium; heat from the gravitative energy of redistributing heavy elements towards the center of the Earth; heat from the tidal friction of slowing the Earth's rotation; and heat from the friction of the grinding edges of the Earth's moving plates.

The accretion of the planets at the time of formation of the solar system generated immense amounts of heat from collision and gravitational collapse. Whether the planets actually melted or not depends on the speed of their accretion, with rapid formation favoring higher temperatures. However, even if the original Earth were molten, the heat of formation alone cannot account for the estimated heat loss from the Earth over its 4.5 billion year life span.

Moreover, even if the Earth had formed cold, the radioactive decay of unstable atoms would have started a warming trend— warming fast at first because of many short-lived, highly radioactive elements, and then more slowly from the longer-lived but less radioactive elements such as uranium 238, thorium 232, and potassium 40. The heat generated from the estimated remainder of these three isotopes in the Earth today can account for all of the world's presently escaping heat (Table 3).

As the primitive Earth was initially being heated by radioactive decay, melting and the gravitational segregation of iron to form the core would have greatly speeded the heating process, perhaps melting the entire Earth. Even so, this gravitational melting would have been a one-shot process and its heat long gone unless sustained by other processes.

TABLE 3
Radioactive heat production from uranium, thorium, and potassium in common igneous rocks

Rock	Amount of radioactive element in rock (parts per million)			Amount of heat produced (joules/kilogram year)
	Uranium	Thorium	Potassium	
Granite	4	13	4	.03
Basalt	0.5	2	1.5	.005
Peridotite	0.02	0.06	0.02	.0001

The heat produced by tidal friction gets its energy from the slowing down of the Earth's rotation. (Some studies on the growth bands of 400-million-year-old fossil corals indicate that a year may once have had more than 400 days.) Much of this energy is dissipated in the swirling tides of the Earth's oceans, but some geologists believe that the tidal warping of weak zones inside the solid Earth may be another continuing source of heat.

As in many geologic debates, the problem is complicated by too many plausible explanations. Probably more than one of the various theoretical sources of energy are involved, and all of them are virtually inexhaustible in terms of human time spans.

Regardless of the exact source of the heat in the Earth, much is known about the variation of temperature near the surface. In deep mines and drill holes, the temperature increases with depth. The rate of increase, called the thermal gradient, averages about 30°C per kilometer of depth. By measuring the heat-insulating quality of rocks, which is quite high, the actual loss of heat from inside the Earth can be calculated. This quantity is about 5000 times less than the heat that reaches the Earth from the sun. Even so, it is an enormous amount of energy, much larger than the more spectacular heat loss from all of the Earth's volcanoes.

At 30°C per kilometer the 800-to-1200°C melting temperatures of rock should be reached at depths of 30 to 40 kilometers beneath the Earth's surface. However, there is good evidence that the thermal gradient is not steady, but rather that the rate of increase slows at greater depths. This is because of the way the radioactive isotopes of uranium, thorium, and potassium are distributed within the Earth. These elements have an affinity to granitic rocks and tend to be concentrated in the Earth's crust. The production of heat from their radioactive decay therefore diminishes with depth, and this reduces the rate at which temperatures increase with depth. The best estimates of this effect indicate that temperatures inside the Earth reach 800 to 1200°C at depths of 60 to 100 kilometers beneath the surface.

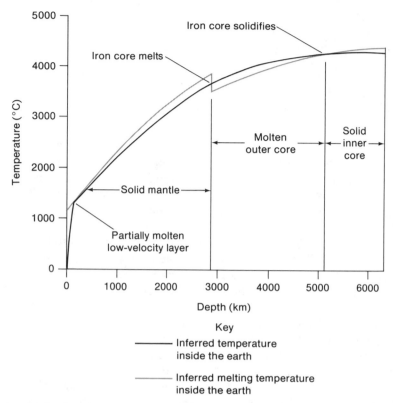

Key

──────── Inferred temperature
inside the earth

──────── Inferred melting temperature
inside the earth

76 Graph of inferred temperature (black line) and inferred melting temperature (gray line) inside the Earth. There are four control points for this graph: (1) The thermal gradient near the Earth's surface is about a 30 °C increase per kilometer of depth. (2) At a depth of about 100 kilometers the actual temperature and melting temperature curves must almost touch to account for the low strength and partial melting of the low-velocity layer. (3) For the lower mantle to be solid and the upper outer core molten, the actual temperature and melting temperature curves must cross. (4) For the lower outer core to be molten and the upper inner core to be solid, the actual temperature and melting temperature curves must again cross. (Data from J. Verhoogen, D.L. Anderson, G. Kennedy, and G. Higgins.)

This is the same depth as the top of the seismic low-velocity layer described in Chapter 1—an important point of independent evidence supporting the temperature calculations. The roots of volcanoes must then extend down at least 60 to 100 kilometers beneath the surface to reach a source of magma (Figure 76).

Seismic evidence indicates that the low-velocity layer is not a zone of completely liquid melt. Rather, the magma is only partially molten; perhaps a few percent of the total material is liquid and is contained in a spongelike mass of weak but solid rock at high temperature. How then does the magma separate and ascend towards the surface?

The density of magma is less than that of the rock from which it melts. Under the influence of gravity the lighter molten rock tends to rise, and the residual solid rock to sink. Any fractures reaching deep into the Earth would hasten this upward movement of magma, which would tend to escape in the same manner as petroleum gushes from a wild well. The problem is the conduit. Do fractures reach down through the rigid crust into the melt zone, or do bodies of magma push and melt their way slowly upward as great rising blobs to feed the shallow magma chambers?

Separating plate margins have major fractures, and volcanoes along the mid-ocean ridges probably have conduits along these fractures between the plates. In these rift zones the thermal gradients are much higher than average, and seismic evidence indicates that the low-velocity layer comes up to within 10 or 20 kilometers of the surface.

In island arc volcanoes at converging plate margins, the volcanoes occur in belts parallel to the marginal thrust faults but are offset about 100 kilometers onto the overriding plate. It is not clear if this is a special fracture zone along which magma can ascend, or if the extra magma generated along the thrust surface forces its own way upward (Figure 77).

In Hawaii the location of earthquakes below the shallow magma chamber of Kilauea indicates that there is a cylindrical zone of fractures about 5 kilometers in diameter and from 10 to 50 kilometers deep, reaching down to the top of the low-velocity layer. The shape of this region of active cracking does not imply a major fracture zone parallel to the Hawaiian Island Chain, but rather a local zone of failure closely associated with

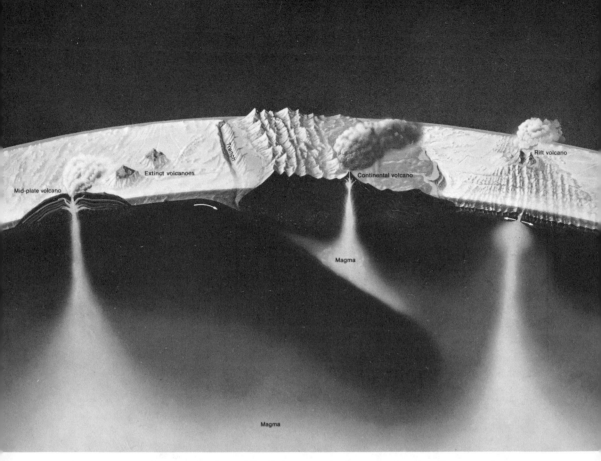

77 Schematic diagram of the three types of volcanoes related to plate tectonic processes. Right: Rift volcanoes formed by separating plates such as submarine volcanoes on the Mid-Atlantic Ridge and Icelandic volcanoes. Center: Volcanoes formed by converging plates at subduction zones such as Japan and the Andes Mountains of South America. Left: Hot-spot volcanoes such as Hawaii and the Hawaiian Ridge. (From *Powers of Nature.* Copyright © 1978, National Geographic Society. All rights reserved.)

the ascending magma. Here it appears that the magma forces its own way up to the shallow magma chamber beneath Kilauea. The rate of inflation of the summit area of Kilauea over the past 20 years indicates that magma is being continuously fed from depth into the magma chamber at 3 to 6 kilometers below the surface, but not at a steady rate (Figure 78).

No one has ever seen the deep roots of volcanoes, but improved geophysical techniques can provide some startling indirect views. In Yellowstone Park, small delays in the transit time of vibrations from distant earthquakes indicate that a large

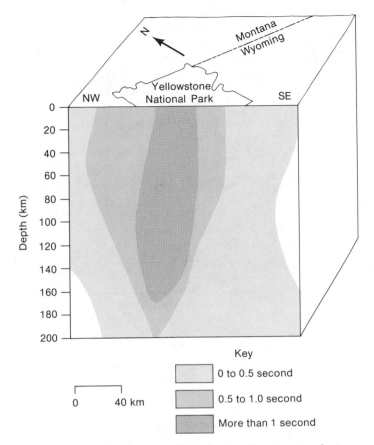

78 Schematic diagram of Yellowstone Park showing the seismic velocity anomaly at depth. Vibrations from distant earthquakes are delayed more than one second during their passage through the region shown. The carrot-shaped zone may include a huge volume of still-molten rock. (Data from H.M. Iyer, U.S. Geological Survey.)

body of magma underlies much of the region. By recording these delays of only a few seconds at many seismograph locations, geophysicists can map the rough size and shape of the huge magma chamber (Figure 78).

Another seismic technique, a spin-off from prospecting for oil by the reflections of sound waves generated at the surface, extends the "x-ray vision" of geophysicists to a depth of 50 kilometers. Analysis of the deep seismic cross sections obtained by this technique reveals a great deal of complexity in

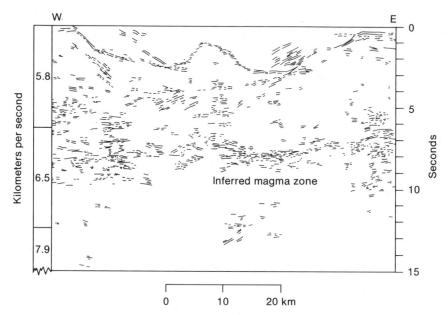

79 Deep seismic-reflection profile beneath the Rio Grande Valley near Socorro, New Mexico. The short lines indicate the apparent distance down to layers that echo strong vibrations generated at the surface. The left-hand scale shows the velocity of the seismic waves in kilometers per second. The right-hand scale shows the time delay between the signal and the echo. The base of the sedimentary rocks filling the valley is shown by the line of reflections at delay times of 1 to 3 seconds (depths of 3 to 6 kilometers). The zone of reflections with about 7 seconds delay time (depth 20 kilometers) is interpreted to be the top of a layer of molten rock. (After S. Schilt and others, *Reviews of Geophysics and Space Physics* 17, 1979, p. 359. Copyright © 1979, American Geophysical Union. All rights reserved.)

the rock structures at depth. In the Rio Grande Rift section in New Mexico, a major sound-reflecting zone at about 20 kilometers beneath the surface is thought to be a layer of magma (Figure 79).

For geologists and volcanologists who are getting their first geophysical look at magma, these are exciting times.

Opposite. Sea, sky, and steam: Hawaiian lava flow enters the ocean. (Photograph by G.A. Macdonald, U.S. Geological Survey.)

11
Origin of the Sea and Air

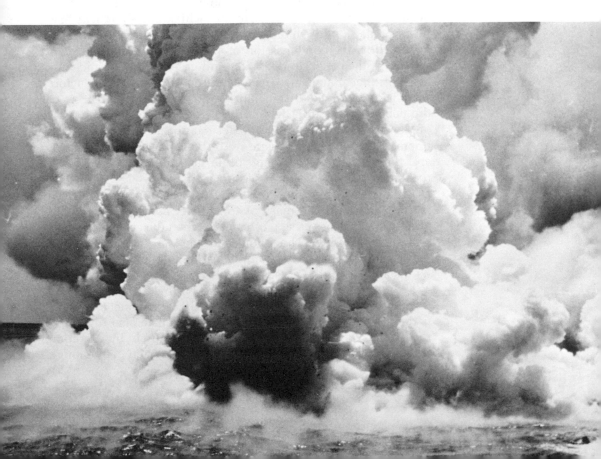

11 Origin of the Sea and Air

The smell of sulphur is strong,
but not unpleasant for a sinner.
Mark Twain   (1866)

Of all the inner planets—Mercury, Venus, Earth and Mars—
only Earth has oceans. Venus has a massive, dense atmosphere
of carbon dioxide and sulphuric acid which hides its rocky face
in perpetual clouds, but its 500°C surface temperature is too
hot to allow the condensation of an ocean.

What is the origin of the water and gases on Earth, and why
are the inner planets so diverse in this respect? Many factors
seem to be involved: distance from the sun, the composition of
the nebular gases from which the planet condensed, the mass
of the planet, the presence or absence of an original atmosphere, the changing temperature of the interior of the planet,
and the amount of water and other gases bound up with the
rocks and metals that form the planet.

The distance from the sun strongly affects a planet's surface
temperature, and the mass of the planet controls its field of
gravity. Light gases escape into space when the surface is warm
and the gravity low. The moon's surface is a vacuum for these
reasons; it does not have enough mass to hold an atmosphere at
its distance from the sun.

The question of how much of the Earth's atmosphere was
there originally—that is, formed at the time the planet formed—
is the basis of a controversial and lively debate also involving
the role of volcanoes. If the Earth formed slowly by accretion
from a nebular dust cloud, it may have remained cool enough

for an original atmosphere to form. By contrast, if there was rapid hot accretion or if surface temperatures were higher than at present because of either internal processes such as radioactive heating or external processes such as excessive heat from the early ignition of the sun, any original atmosphere would have boiled away.

The "neon argument" supports the concept of loss or lack of any original atmosphere. Neon is an inert gas; it does not combine with silicate minerals or metals to form solid compounds. Neon is also relatively abundant as a gas in the cosmos, and its physical properties indicate that it is not subject to loss into space from the Earth's present atmosphere. Any original atmosphere of the Earth derived from a cosmic dust cloud should have had a modest amount of neon in it. But the Earth's present atmosphere has only a trivial fraction of neon, much less than that expected in an original atmosphere. The lack of neon indicates that the original neon was lost along with all the other gases and water from the hot surface of some primitive Earth. A later atmosphere and oceans evolving from volcanic gases escaping to the Earth's surface would not include neon. Only gases such as water, carbon dioxide, and others that could be chemically bound into solid matter would be released by melting and eruption on the Earth's surface.

For these reasons, most geologists and astronomers think the Earth's oceans and atmosphere have been boiled and sweated out of the solid Earth over long periods of time; that the seas and air have accumulated during the evolution of the Earth rather than having formed in the beginning.

This brings us back to volcanoes, for they are the vents that release the gases trapped in the rocks of the Earth's interior. Molten basalt rising to the Earth's surface contains about 0.5 percent by weight of dissolved gases. These gases are in solution in the same way that carbon dioxide gas is dissolved in beer. They exsolve and effervesce into gas bubbles and foam as the magma reaches the surface, just as beer foams when its pressure is suddenly released.

It is not easy to determine the composition of volcanic gases, since they escape during eruptions. Huge volumes of gases are involved in explosive eruptions, but it is virtually impossible to get close enough to sample them before they mix and react with unknown amounts of air. Indirect methods of sampling have proved more successful. Gases in deep submarine eruptions are frozen into the glassy rinds of pillow lavas. These trapped gases have been analyzed by James Moore of the U.S. Geological Survey, who has provided some of the best estimates of the composition of volcanic gases currently available.

Sometimes crystals forming in a cooling magma chamber will enclose a tiny pocket of melt. If these crystals are erupted, the melt pocket quenches to an inclusion of glass in which the volcanic gases are trapped. Analysis of these inclusions by Fred Anderson at the University of Chicago has revealed that subduction volcanoes have a much higher gas content than submarine rift volcanoes.

Richard Stoiber of Dartmouth College has pioneered still other techniques for analyzing volcanic gases. He uses instruments called absorbtion spectrometers to measure the sulfur dioxide (SO_2) in volcanic fume clouds backlighted by the sky; he also analyzes gases adsorbed on volcanic ash particles collected as they fall from the eruption clouds. His studies indicate that each active volcano generates about as much sulfur gas pollution as a major coal-fired electric power station.

The sum of these studies allows some reasonable estimates of the volume and composition of the volcanic gases currently being added to the water and air budget of the Earth. By numbers of atoms, hydrogen is the most important constituent of volcanic gas followed by oxygen, carbon, sulfur, chlorine, and nitrogen. As the elements combine at the surface conditions on the Earth they become water (H_2O), carbon dioxide (CO_2), sulfur dioxide (SO_2), hydrochloric acid (HCl), and nitrogen (N_2). The ratios of these volcanic gases are in remarkable accord with the ratios of water, carbon, chlorine, and nitrogen in the air, oceans, and surficial rocks of the Earth. However, the ratio of sulfur is not.

80 Volcanic gases escaping from this crack in the cinder cone formed during the Kilauea Iki eruption in Hawaii are depositing an encrustation of minerals. Wayne Ault of the Hawaiian Volcano Observatory measures the temperature of the vent and collects gas for chemical analysis. (Photograph by the U.S. Geological Survey.)

Although the compositional ratios appear generally correct for a volcanic source of the Earth's air and water, what about the total amounts of these gases? Rifting of the plates produces about 2.5 square kilometers of new area on the Earth's surface each year. This scar is filled by submarine lava flows and shallow intrusive rocks down to depths of approximately 5 kilometers, producing a total of 12 to 13 cubic kilometers of new volcanic rock each year. Estimates for subduction volcanoes are only 1 to 2 cubic kilometers of new volcanic products per year, and hot spot volcanoes produce less than 1 cubic kilometer per year. Thus, the simplest model is to multiply the 13 cubic kilometers of rift volcanic products by the percentages of gases in submarine basalts by the 4.5-billion-year age of the Earth, and ignore the smaller contribution from subduction and hot spot volcanoes (Figure 81). Of course, most of the gases in submarine lavas do not escape during eruptions, but are trapped in the rock by the high pressure of the overlying sea water. These gases are released gradually as the crust of the seafloor cools and reacts with sea water during its 100-to-200-million-year trip across the ocean to its grave in some future subduction zone.

The results of this calculation of the total volume of volcanic gases indicate that the present rate of volcanic activity can account for only 25 percent of the water, carbon, chlorine, and nitrogen at the Earth's surface. This discrepancy can be explained in two ways. Perhaps volcanism was more intense in the geologic past than at present. Many geologists believe there was an early period of extreme volcanic activity caused by the heating of the Earth from now depleted radioactive elements and by gravitational heat released when the Earth's metallic core was formed.

The other explanation is to assume that there is some unknown reason for the lack of neon in an original atmosphere and to infer that 75 percent of our present oceans and atmosphere has existed since the Earth's beginning.

Sulfur appears to be a special problem. Even at the present rate of emission from volcanoes, there should be 50 times more

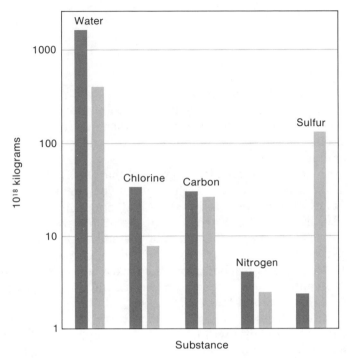

81 Comparison of volatile molecules and elements in the Earth's oceans and atmosphere to their volcanic production. (Note logarithmic scale.) For each substance, the bar on the left represents the total weight of that material in the air, oceans, and sedimentary rocks of the Earth. The bar on the right represents the weight of that same substance currently being produced from volcanoes multiplied by the age of the Earth. Greater volcanic output in past ages is required if volcanoes have been the only source of water, chlorine, carbon, and nitrogen. It is also apparent that some process such as subduction must remove sulfur from the Earth's surface.

sulfur at the Earth's surface. What has saved us from the sulfuric acid blanket that plagues the planet Venus? The answer is probably iron sulfide (FeS)—the pyrites (or "fools gold") that form a common mineral—and also the plate tectonic process. Instead of being released into the ocean or atmosphere, sulfur reacts with iron and forms insoluble FeS which stays in the oceanic crust and is returned via a subduction zone to the shallow interior of the Earth.

The possibility that sulfur is scavenged from the Earth's surface by the seafloor-spreading machine has spawned a new school of thought championed by William Fyfe of the University of Western Ontario in Canada. Fyfe points out that perhaps more water is being consumed in the water-rich rocks entering subduction zones than is being returned to the surface in volcanic gases.

This idea reverses the classic concept that the Earth has been releasing gases to the surface throughout geologic time. In this new view, a primitive Earth had a thick atmosphere and universal ocean which covered solid rocks of low water and gas content. The stirring of this Earth by plate tectonics caused the surface water and gases to mix down into the mantle rocks of the Earth, perhaps scrubbing out the excess sulfur in the process. The entire idea is so new and so contrary to the classical concept that the solid Earth loses gases with time, that its geochemical implications are still making waves. If it turns out to be true, volcanologists will have to be content to think that our present volcanoes merely recycle the air and oceans instead of creating them.

Either way, the marvel is the delicate balance between volcanism and tectonism over an immense span of time that has kept the Earth—perhaps alone among the planets—hospitable to life.

12

Volcanic Power

12 Volcanic Power

Fires that shook me once, but now to silent
  ashes fall'n away
Cold upon the dead volcano sleeps the gleam of
  dying day.
Tennyson (1809–1892)

Geothermal energy was a phrase known to only a few special-
ists until the 1974 energy crisis. Now, although not exactly a
household name, it has become a familiar term for an alterna-
tive source of energy.

In discussing geothermal energy and power, it is important
to understand the subtle difference between these terms. Heat
is a form of energy, and there is an immense amount of it inside
the Earth. For each kilometer of depth the temperature increases about 20 to 60°C, depending on the region (Figure 82).
The heat energy contained in just the upper 10 kilometers of
the United States is estimated to be 3.3×10^{25} joules. If it were
accessible, it would supply our energy needs for the next
100,000 years.

But potential energy becomes practical only when it can be
consumed at some useful rate. Power is a measure of the *rate* at
which energy is made available or is consumed. Energy is
measured in joules. Power is measured in joules per second or
watts. There is plenty of diffuse energy in the Earth; turning it
into useful power is the critical problem.

The difference between energy and power becomes clear in
the following examples: The amount of solar energy is enormous, but the solar power reaching Earth is modest—averaging
about 40 watts for each square meter of surface. A lightning
bolt contains only a modest amount of energy, equal to that of
about two barrels of crude oil, but it expends this energy in a
fraction of a second, unleashing enormous power.

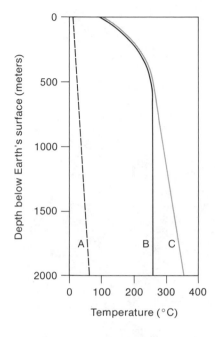

82 Temperatures beneath the Earth's surface in regions of hot springs and geysers are distinctly different from those in more normal regions (Curve A). Curve B is typical of temperatures in a geyser basin or geothermal steam field. Curve C is the temperature of boiling water under hydrostatic pressures at various depths. (After D.E. White, U.S. Geological Survey.)

Volcanic explosions are often incorrectly compared to nuclear bombs. Although the heat and mechanical energy in the 1883 eruption of Krakatau was in the order of 5000 megatons of TNT, this energy was released in a series of explosions lasting about one day. A nuclear bomb goes off in a single almost instantaneous flash unleashing power in amounts unmatched by geological phenomena.

Geothermal energy, like solar energy, is enormous, but its natural rate of release is trivial—averaging about 1/16 watt from beneath each square meter of the Earth's surface. Even if one could convert geothermal energy to electricity with an efficiency of 20 percent, it would require all of the heat flow from an area as large as a football field to power a 60-watt light bulb. Only in a few volcanic regions like Yellowstone, New Zealand, and Iceland, where geysers and hot springs are abundant, does nature sustain a significant output of geothermal power.

For geothermal power to be practical, some special situation must exist that can concentrate the Earth's heat energy into a small area. Natural or artificial underground reservoirs of steam or hot water that can be funneled into a drillhole provide this special situation (Figure 83).

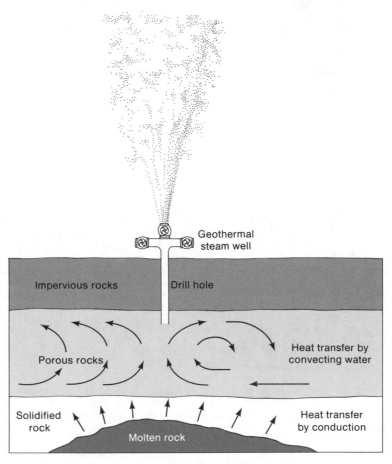

83 Schematic diagram of a geothermal power reservoir.

In nonvolcanic areas, drill holes to depths of 6 or 7 kilometers just reach boiling temperatures. However, in young volcanic regions, where molten rock has brought heat up from deeper levels, it is possible to drill into rocks and steam reservoirs heated to 100 to 350°C or hotter at depths of 1 to 3 kilometers. To develop the true potential of geothermal power it is necessary to locate these shallow bodies of hot rocks and fluids, and to tap their pent-up energy with a system of drill holes.

Exploring for geothermal power is similar to exploring for oil, except that the geologic setting is volcanic rather than sedimentary. All the existing geothermal power fields have been found in active or young volcanic regions.

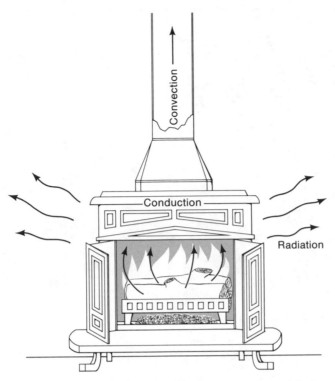

84 Sketch of woodstove shows heat transfer by convection of the heated air and wood smoke in the stove; by conduction through the firebrick and iron walls of the stove; and by radiation from the surface of the stove through the open space of the room.

The form of heat transfer in a given region is of key importance. Heat is transferred by radiation, conduction, and convection. Radiation transfers a significant amount of heat through transparent media like air and space, but it is much less effective in solids. Conduction is such a slow process in good thermal insulators like rocks that only small amounts of heat are transferred inside the Earth by conduction. The very slow release of the Earth's interior heat through its surface (averaging 0.06 watt per square meter) is controlled by this slow conduction process.

Convection is the only process rapid enough to transfer the Earth's heat at rates sufficient to produce significant power. Convection involves the actual physical movement of molten rocks or hot fluids, generally upward, because these hot rocks and fluids are less dense than their surrounding cooler media (Figure 84).

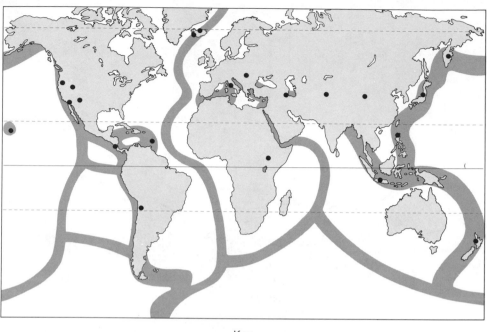

Key

Regions favorable for geothermal prospecting

● Location of geothermal power plants

85 Map of geothermal regions of the world. Notice the close relationship to zones of active volcanoes.

Geothermal power fields occur where magma has moved upward from depths of 50 to 100 kilometers and brought the high temperatures (900 to 1200°C) of these depths to near the surface. Ground water heated by these volcanic intrusions can form another convection circuit bringing hot springs and geysers to the very surface, or remaining sealed below the surface awaiting the wildcatter's drill.

Geothermal prospects related to volcanic activity are of three types: hydrothermal reservoirs, hot dry rocks, and magma reservoirs. Of the three, the hydrothermal reservoirs are the easiest to develop because their hot water and steam are waiting to be tapped (Figure 85).

Larderello, Italy is an area of natural hot springs. The high boric acid content in these thermal waters has been extracted for over 200 years. Wells drilled to increase chemical produc-

86 Larderello, Italy is the site of the world's first geothermal steam field. Started in 1904, it now produces about 300 to 400 megawatts of electricity. The huge chimneys are cooling towers similar to those used at nuclear power plants for recycling the cooling water. (Photograph by Patrick Muffler, U.S. Geological Survey.)

tion encountered steam, and were first used to produce electricity in 1904. Some 300 wells to depths of 300 to 700 meters have been drilled over the years and have outlined a producing steam reservoir at 235°C and 30 bars of pressure. The reservoir is in porous limestone, but young volcanic rocks in the area are considered to be the heat source. The field has produced some 400 megawatts of power over the last 30 years and is still going strong (Figure 86).

Icelanders began to drill for hot water and steam in 1925. By now they have developed over 250 fields whose power is used mainly for space heating. Some 70 percent of Reykjavík, the capital city of 100,000 people, gets its heat and hot water from 110 wells, 300 to 2200 meters deep, that tap water at about 100°C in porous basalts. Although once flowing wells now need to be pumped, the temperatures have shown no decrease.

87 *Geysir* is an Icelandic word meaning to gush, but the Great Geysir of Haukadalur, the world's original, seldom performs. Its small neighbor, Strokkur Geysir, seen in this photograph, erupts every few minutes.

For the people in oil-barren, arctic Iceland, geothermal power is the very life blood of their warmth and comfort.

The Geysers, California, a region of young volcanic rocks in the Coast Range of California north of San Francisco, was drilled for steam in 1921. Electricity was first generated in 1959 and the power field has been steadily expanded since that time. Over 100 wells, 500 to 2600 meters deep, produce steam at 240°C and 30 bars of pressure from a reservoir of fractured

88 The Geysers, California, once a hot spring health spa, is now the world's largest geothermal steam field. Producing 500 megawatts and still expanding, the field generates enough electricity to supply San Francisco. (Photograph by Pacific Gas and Electric Company.)

shaley sandstone. The production has recently been expanded to 500 megawatts, enough electricity for San Francisco. It is the largest geothermal electrical generating installation in the world and is still growing (Figure 88). The Geysers is an exceptionally valuable geothermal field; the power produced there is low cost and trouble free, making it the shining light of geothermal prospectors.

On the Island of Hawaii, a recently drilled geothermal exploration well has encountered some of the hottest underground fluids yet found. Drilled into lava flows on the East Rift of Kilauea Volcano to a depth of 1969 meters, the hole has a bottom temperature of 350°C. Steam production tests indicate that this single well has an electrical generating potential of about 3

89 First geothermal steam well in Hawaii is located on the east rift of Kilauea Volcano. A 3-megawatt electrical generator is now being installed on this well. (Photograph by Larry Kadooka, *Hawaii Tribune Herald*.)

megawatts (Figure 89). However, the size of the reservoir has not yet been determined.

The prospects for generating geothermal power from hot dry rocks are more speculative. These potential fields involve areas of higher-than-normal thermal gradients on the order of 60°C per kilometer of depth in areas of impermeable rocks. Drill holes to 3-or-4-kilometer depths can reach down into these hot dry rocks. Artificial fractures are established between two closely spaced holes and cold surface water is pumped down an injection well. Heated by the hot rock along the fractures, it rises as hot water or steam in a return well (Figure 90).

Los Alamos Scientific Laboratory in New Mexico is actually performing this experiment on the flank of the Valles caldera. Cold water pumped down one 3-kilometer-deep well returns up another at 135°C. The key question not yet answered is the

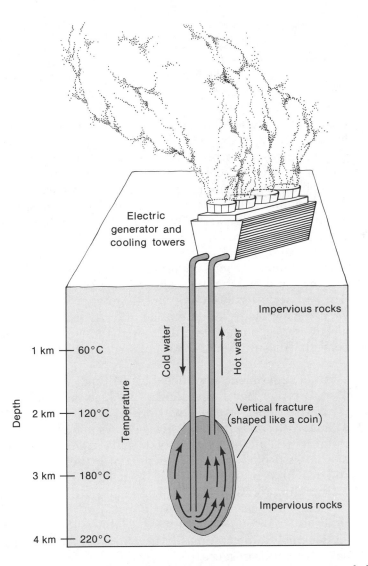

Electric generator and cooling towers

Impervious rocks

Cold water

Hot water

Vertical fracture (shaped like a coin)

Impervious rocks

Depth

Temperature

1 km — 60°C

2 km — 120°C

3 km — 180°C

4 km — 220°C

90 Schematic diagram of the Hot Dry Rock geothermal power concept. Two holes are drilled into impervious rocks in regions where the temperature increases rapidly with depth. The holes are connected by hydraulic fracturing, a process of fracturing rock by pumping high fluid pressure down a well. Surface water is injected into one hole; it gets heated from contact with hot rocks at depth, and rises in the second hole as hot water or steam. Cooling of the rocks at depth causes further fracturing, allowing the circulating water to reach additional hot surfaces. Preliminary tests near Los Alamos, New Mexico with wells drilled to a depth of 3 kilometers in granite at 200°C have been encouraging.

nature of the fractured rock at depth. If the cooling of the buried rock mass will lead to a volume reduction and more fracturing of still hot rocks, as the experimenters hope, then the wells should produce enough power for commercial use. By contrast, if no new cracks form, the original fractures will soon cool and the amount of power produced will decline too rapidly to pay for the drilling costs.

The process of artificially making a geothermal reservoir within hot buried rocks is a difficult and expensive experiment, but if successful, the potential is enormous. Much of the young mountian terrain in the western United States, as well as in Hawaii and Alaska, is of volcanic origin and forms a tempting but well-locked buried treasure of geothermal energy.

Even molten rock itself is a potential source of power. Magma contains about 1000 joules of heat energy per gram. The energy in 1 cubic kilometer of magma is enough to light San Francisco for 200 years. But tapping it requires truly advanced technology; although scientifically it is probably feasible to extract power directly from shallow bodies of magma beneath volcanic centers, the engineering technology is still years away.

Initial experiments conducted by drilling into buried masses of molten rock have been done on Kilauea Iki lava lake in Hawaii. This great lake of lava formed during an eruption of Kilauea Volcano in 1959 when lava flows ponded in an ancient crater to a depth of 100 meters. Lava is such a good insulator that holes drilled in 1979 to depths of below 50 meters were still reaching near molten rock in Kilauea Iki. Conventional rock drilling techniques using abundant water to keep the drill bit cool have been successful in reaching the molten rock. However, efforts to emplace devices down the holes into the molten rock to determine the feasibility of extracting energy have not yet been successful.

Even though geothermal power is still an infant and largely unproved industry, its potential makes it worth serious effort and investment. The U.S. Geological Survey in a recent assessment of potential geothermal energy resources in the fifty states to depths of 10 kilometers listed the following estimates: hydrothermal reservoirs, 12×10^{21} joules, or about 2 times the

91 Old Faithful geyser in Yellowstone National Park has erupted every 40 to 80 minutes for the past 100 years. Spraying 50,000 kilograms of boiling water 35 to 50 meters high, each eruption releases about 1.9×10^8 joules of energy during its few minutes duration (about 1 megawatt of power.) Thick deposits of silica precipitated from the cooling waters indicate that the Yellowstone geyser basins have been active for thousands of years.

energy in the world's oil reserves; hot dry rock, 32×10^{24} joules, or about 6000 times the energy in the world's oil reserves; magma reservoirs, 4×10^{23} joules, or about 80 times the energy in the world's oil reserves.

In our view, volcanoes, directly and indirectly, are powerhouses of enormous potential. The most scenic, such as Yellowstone, Kilauea, and others in National Parks should never be developed. But others may help to provide light and warmth in centuries to come. It will take a major research and engineering effort involving much time, labor, and money to find out. Like all human adventures, high payoff involves high risk.

13

Volcanic Treasures

13 Volcanic Treasures

But see the mountain
Shaking with the waves of heat
Where day has gone.
Onitsura   (1661–1738)

Volcanoes are nature's forges and stills where the elements of the Earth, both rare and common, are moved and sorted. Some elements are diluted and some pass through unchanged, but many are transported and concentrated into those precious lodes that people seek for fortune or industry.

Economically important elements concentrated directly by volcanic action, especially by the intrusion of magma bodies into the Earth's crust, include fluorine, sulfur, zinc, copper, lead, arsenic, tin, molybdenum, uranium, tungsten, silver, mercury, and gold. These concentrations are mainly formed as hydrothermal vein deposits, which are the mineral fillings precipitated from hot waters percolating along underground fractures. Veins generally consist of one or more common minerals, like quartz (SiO_2) or calcite ($CaCO_3$), in which the more precious minerals, like gold (Au) or galena (lead sulfide, PbS), are scattered as small specks or crystals.

Theoretically the process is simple, but in operation it can be enormously complex. Basically, the magmatic roots of volcanoes supply the heat source and perhaps some of the ingredients for a giant still. As the magma cools and the common silicate minerals crystallize to form basalt or granite, the water and other gases, as well as the rarer elements that don't fit into the rock-forming silicate minerals, become concentrated in the residual liquid magma. As the cooling reduces the volume of the rocks, they crack, allowing the hot residual magmatic fluids,

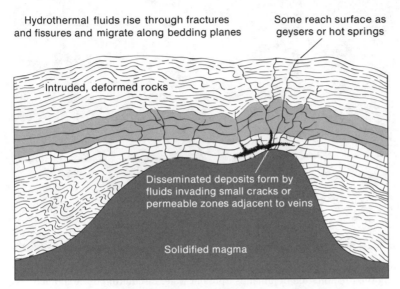

Hydrothermal fluids rise through fractures and fissures and migrate along bedding planes

Some reach surface as geysers or hot springs

Intruded, deformed rocks

Disseminated deposits form by fluids invading small cracks or permeable zones adjacent to veins

Solidified magma

92 Ore deposits are often found in close proximity to an intrusion of solidified magma. Many such deposits probably precipitate out of the hot waters associated with the cooling magma. (From F. Press and R. Siever, *Earth*, Second Edition, p. 577. W.H. Freeman and Company, Copyright © 1978.)

rich in water and precious elements, to escape from their underground forge. During the ascent of these hydrothermal solutions toward the surface, cooling and decreasing pressure cause various minerals, both common and rare, to precipitate and form veins. Certain minerals precipitate over a large range of pressure and temperature and are common throughout the vein; others such as gold and silver may precipitate over a very narrow range of pressure and temperature to form localized bonanzas within the vein (Figure 92).

Veins are usually steeply inclined ledges dipping into the Earth, a few centimeters to many meters thick, and often many hundreds of meters or several kilometers in length (Figure 93). The goldbearing veins of the Mother Lode system in the Sierra

93 Outcropping vein of quartz about 1 meter thick in Yavapai County, Arizona. Veins are formed by the precipitation of minerals from hot water circulating through fractures. Some veins contain precious minerals; others are barren. (Photograph by F.C. Canney, U.S. Geological Survey.)

foothills of California trend north–south and dip steeply down toward the granite roots of the range. Although each vein is generally no more than a meter or so thick and a few kilometers long, the vein system crops out for over 300 kilometers in the western Sierra Nevada. Hot waters escaping through steep cracks from the volcanic roots of the range deposited mainly hard, milky-white quartz in the veins, with few (but enough) specks of gold and pyrites (FeS_2, fool's gold) to start the rush to California.

The type of rock surrounding the cooling magma reservoir is of key importance in the formation of ore deposits. In Hawaii (in fact in almost all oceanic volcanic islands) ore deposits are nearly nonexistent. Part of the reason for this may be that most oceanic islands are slowly sinking from their own enormous load, thus hiding any ore deposits that have formed. But even in the unusual case where uplift and erosion have exposed the

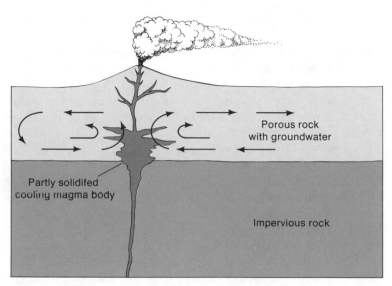

Porous rock
with groundwater

Partly solidifed
cooling magma body

Impervious rock

94 Schematic diagram of groundwater being circulated by the cooling of a magma body. The water seeps into the cooling magma body, is heated, and convects upward. Reaching cooler rocks above the magma body, the circulating groundwater also cools and precipitates vein minerals. The source of the minerals may be either the magma or the porous rock through which the groundwater circulates. In this model, the cooling magma body acts as a circulating pump and concentrator, rather than as a direct source of ore deposits.

roots of volcanic islands, hydrothermal ore deposits are rare or absent. Many geologists believe that this is because the rocks surrounding the magmatic roots of volcanoes are the true source of the valuable elements found in hydrothermal veins. According to this view, the volcanic rocks act as a heat source that pumps existing groundwater into a giant circulating system. Cold waters, being heavier, move down and into the cooling volcanic rocks carrying trace quantities of valuable elements leached from the surrounding rocks. Heated by the cooling magma, they become less dense and rise into the fractured rocks above. Cooling and losing pressure again, they precipitate their quartz and precious ores into the veins forming above the volcanic hearth (Figure 94).

Mercury, copper, sulfur, and fluorine have been measured in

volcanic gases in Hawaii, so there is no question that at least some of these elements originate directly in volcanoes. Gold, silver, and other valuable elements found in hydrothermal ore deposits may have to be preconcentrated in some earlier generation of continental crustal rocks before they can be reconcentrated by volcanic distillation.

Each mineral has its characteristic place in the hydrothermal system. Tungsten minerals precipitate at very high temperatures and often occur at the very point of contact between a chilled magma body and the rocks it has invaded, especially limestone. Scheelite, a calcium tungstate mineral ($CaWO_4$) is brightly fluorescent under ultraviolet light. Tungsten prospectors seek out contacts between granite and limestone during the day, and then prospect these outcrops at night with "blacklights" to reveal the areas of high tungsten concentration.

Mercury is at the other extreme. Both as an element and in compounds, it is volatile; that is, it forms a gas at low temperatures and pressures. For this reason, much of the Earth's mercury is lost to the surface from volcanic steam vents and hot springs. Near many active volcanoes the concentration of mercury in the air exceeds the health standards established by environmental protection agencies. However, it is difficult to get the volcanoes to stop smoking.

Diamonds, perhaps the greatest mineral treasure of all, are also closely related to volcanic processes. Diamonds and the graphite cores of common pencils are the same element—carbon—but they are different minerals. In graphite, the carbon atoms are arranged in layers like mica sheets, and the loose bonding between layers permits the sheets to break and slide past one another. Graphite is therefore soft and greasy feeling. In diamonds, the atoms of carbon are compressed into a tight network that interlocks in all directions, forming the hardest substance known on Earth (Figure 95). To attain this close packing of carbon atoms, extremely high pressures are needed—pressures that occur naturally only at depths of nearly 200 kilometers inside the Earth. Once formed, diamonds are stable at low pressures and temperatures; however they will burn in air at high temperatures.

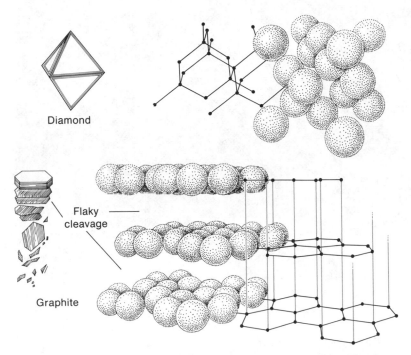

Diamond

Flaky cleavage

Graphite

95 Crystal form and internal structure of diamond and graphite. The three-dimensional network of atomic bonds in diamond make it extremely hard and durable. In contrast, the two-dimensional network of major bonds in graphite make it flaky and soft. (From J. Gilluly, A.C. Waters, and A.O. Woodford, *Principles of Geology*, Fourth Edition, p. 30. W.H. Freeman and Company. Copyright © 1975.)

The right conditions to form diamonds apparently exist beneath the continents at a depth of nearly 200 kilometers and a temperature near that of molten rock. In fact, diamonds might not be all that rare if we could mine them at their deep source. Their occurrence at the Earth's surface results from a rare type of volcanic eruption that transports them rapidly from great depths into shallow vents called Kimberlite pipes (Figure 96). The reduction in pressure and temperature happens so rapidly that the diamonds do not revert to a more normal surface form of carbon such as graphite.

A

96 A. Famous Kimberley Diamond Pipe in South Africa. This volcanic vent was mined over 1000 meters deep before 1908. (Photograph by DeBeers Consolidated Mines Limited.) B. The cross section shows a reconstruction of the pipe prior to erosion, the present ground surface, and the mined-out zone. (Diagram after Arthur Holmes.)

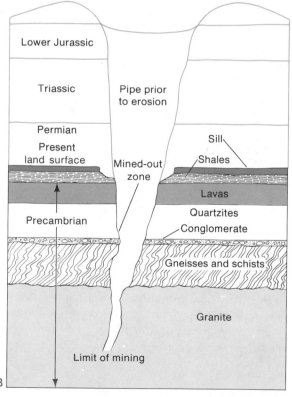

Lower Jurassic

Triassic

Pipe prior
to erosion

Permian

Present
land surface

Mined-out
zone

Sill

Shales

Lavas

Quartzites

Conglomerate

Precambrian

Gneisses and schists

Granite

Limit of mining

B

97 Ol Doinyo Lengai, Mountain of God, in Tanzania, East Africa. The high content of sodium carbonate (washing soda) in lavas from Ol Doinyo Lengai is unique, suggesting that it is related to the type of volcanism which forms diamond pipes. (Photograph by Richard Stoiber.)

It is possible that the type of volcano associated with diamond pipes is not forming today. The peculiar Kimberlite volcanic rock and the presence of other minerals indicating that the volcanic fluids were extremely high in water and carbon dioxide suggest an unusual kind of explosive volcanism that may occur only during certain episodes of geologic history. A few active volcanoes in East Africa, especially those whose rocks are unusually high in carbon dioxide (like Ol Doinyo Lengai), may be the closest active relatives to a diamond-pipe volcano (Figure 97).

Even if they are not emplacing diamonds, most of the world's active volcanoes are probably forming some type of hydrothermal deposits beneath their surface today. This is also true of geothermal reservoirs in which the circulating underground hot water is selectively dissolving, transporting, and depositing the more soluble minerals within the porous rocks. On a geologic time scale, today's volcanoes and geothermal systems may be tomorrow's ore deposits.

The fact that natural geothermal areas like Yellowstone have a life span of ten thousand to hundreds of thousands of years indicates that volcanic ore deposits form quite slowly—drop by drop, atom by atom. People and their machines have voracious appetites for minerals, consuming them at rates far in excess of nature's patient creation. The message here is clear: we must recycle whatever mineral wealth we can or wait eons of time for new supplies.

Opposite. Vesuvius, 1944. (Photograph by the U.S. Navy, courtesy of the National Archives.)

14
Volcanoes and Climate

14 Volcanoes and Climate

*In one period we believe ourselves governed
by immutable laws; in the next by chance.*
Loren Eiseley (1907–1977)

Bad weather has been blamed on almost everything from atomic bombs, sun spots, and the industrial revolution to volcanoes, black magic, the Republicans, and the Democrats. Most bad weather probably results from the natural variability of atmospheric processes, but at least two of the above culprits— volcanoes and the industrial revolution—have put large amounts of debris and gas into the atmosphere, and thus appear more suspect than some of the others.

Benjamin Franklin was the first to suggest that volcanoes modify climate and weather. When Laki Volcano in Iceland erupted in 1783 with the largest effusion of lava in history, an enormous amount of gas was released (Figure 98). A blue haze or "dry fog" enveloped Iceland and much of northern Europe for months. The gas must have contained a significant amount of fluorine because livestock grazing on contaminated grass in Iceland died of fluoridosis. The widespread death of livestock—11,000 cattle; 28,000 horses; and 190,000 sheep— resulted in a severe famine in which 10,000 Icelanders, one-fifth of the population, perished. The "dry fog" reaching Europe was more annoying than poisonous, but it was prevalent on many days during the summer and fall of 1783 and was apparently observed by Franklin during his stay in France.

98 Cinder cones along the Laki fissure in Iceland. This 25-kilometer-long fissure erupted in 1783 with the greatest lava flood in recorded history—12 cubic kilometers spread over more than 500 square kilometers. The gases released during this enormous eruption caused a blue haze or "dry fog" which reached Europe.

Since the winter of 1783–1784 was abnormally severe, especially in Europe, Franklin suggested that fine ash and gases from the Laki eruption may have filtered out enough of the sun's rays to cause the cold weather.

The idea surfaced again after the eruption of Krakatau 100 years later. This time, the visible atmospheric effects were unquestionably worldwide; they began within two weeks of the great explosive eruption and lasted for months. Strange colors and halos of the sun and moon were noted, and there were

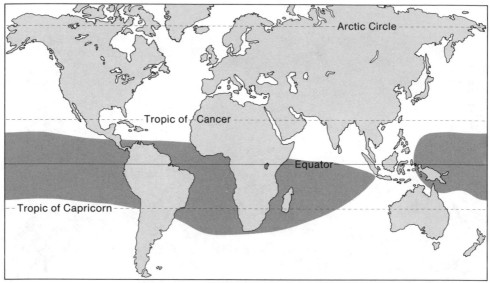

A

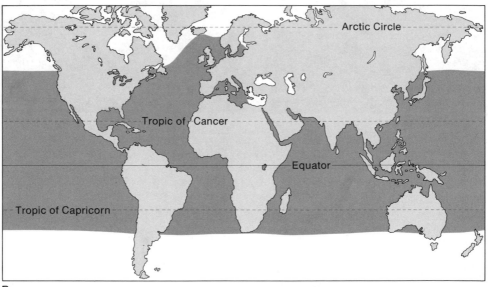

B

99 A. Approximate distribution of sky phenomena between August 26 and September 7, 1883. B. Approximate limits of the main sky phenomena at the end of November 1883. High-speed stratospheric winds averaging nearly 120 kilometers per hour carried the fine volcanic dust of the 1883 Krakatau eruption westward around the globe. By the end of November, the stratospheric haze covered over 70 percent of the Earth's surface causing spectacular sunsets and strange optical phenomena. (After C.J. Symons, ed., *The Eruption of Krakatoa*. Royal Society Report of the Krakatoa Committee, 1888.)

vivid sunrises and sunsets for months on end (Figure 99). A Ceylon newspaper for September 17, 1883 gave this account:

> The sun for the last three days rises in a splendid green when he is visible; about 10° above the horizon. As he advances he assumes a beautiful blue, and as he comes further on looks a brilliant blue, resembling burning sulfur. . . even at the zenith, the light is blue, varying from pale blue to a light blue later on, somewhat similar to moonlight. . . . Then as he declines, the sun assumes the same changes, but vice versa.

Solar radiation decreased 10 percent over the next three years in Europe, and average world temperatures appeared to be below normal (Figure 100). At this point, however, the data become questionable. Most weather observations in the 1880s were made in Europe, and critics of the theory of volcanic influences on weather and climate point out that while Europe was colder, South America may have been warmer, and thus the true average world effects were not known.

Nevertheless, the theory has been tenacious. Harry Wexler, once head of the U.S. Weather Bureau, was a strong proponent of the idea. In 1952 he suggested that the warming trend of

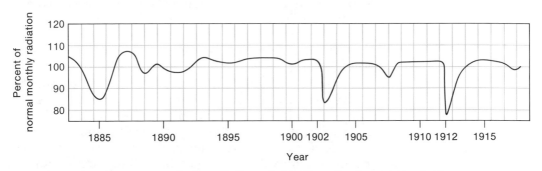

100 Average monthly intensity of solar radiation at the Earth's surface from 1883 to 1918 in relation to normal monthly values. Reductions of 10 to 20 percent occur after the eruptions of Krakatau in 1883, Pelée, Soufrière, and Santa Maria in 1902; and Katmai in 1912. (After Kimball, *Monthly Weather Review* 46, 1918, p. 355.)

world temperatures since 1900 might be caused by the lack of major volcanic eruptions in the first half of the twentieth century. By contrast, he blamed the colder decades closing the nineteenth century on a series of major eruptions: Krakatau in 1883; Tarawera in New Zealand, 1886; Bandai-San in Japan, 1888; and Bogoslof in Alaska, 1890 (Figure 101).

H.H. Lamb, a British climatologist, has also been a champion of the concept that volcanic activity affects climate. He compiled a detailed list of volcanic eruptions since 1500 A.D. and computed a "dust veil index" based on the apparent amount of volcanic debris scattered into the atmosphere. He concluded that there has been a definite relationship between world climatic trends and large volcanic eruptions.

Recently, J.P. Kennett and R.C. Thunell, working with cores from deep-sea-drilling projects, have concluded that the amount of volcanic ash in seafloor sediments increased about 2 million years ago and has stayed high since then. The period of the last 2 million years coincides with the Pleistocene ice ages, and Kennett and Thunell conclude that the extra volcanism and extra cold are not just a coincidence. But even this evidence is not conclusive; some scientists point out that not enough sea cores of the older sediments have yet been taken to make a valid comparison.

If volcanic gas and dust do alter weather and climate, the effect probably operates in the stratosphere (above 10 kilometers) where the layer of haze hovers for a long time because there are no clouds and rain to wash it away quickly (Figure 102). Meteorologists have identified a long-lasting stratospheric aerosol layer at heights of 15 to 30 kilometers that seems to be composed of a thin haze of small particles or droplets, smaller than .001 millimeter in diameter. These particles are composed of various materials including sea salt, silicate dust, and sulfuric acid. They probably originate from several sources—sea spray, dust storms, volcanic eruptions, forest fires, industrial smoke stacks, and so on. The density of the

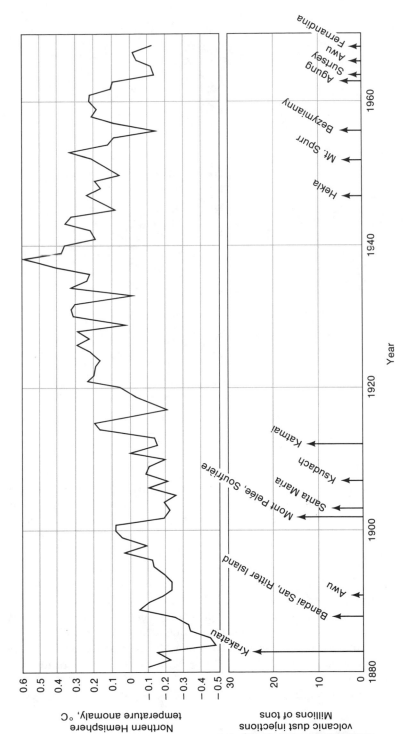

101 Graph of average temperature variations in the northern hemisphere and major volcanic eruptions that injected dust into the stratosphere. (After Robert Oliver, *Journal of Applied Meteorology* 15, 1976, p. 934.)

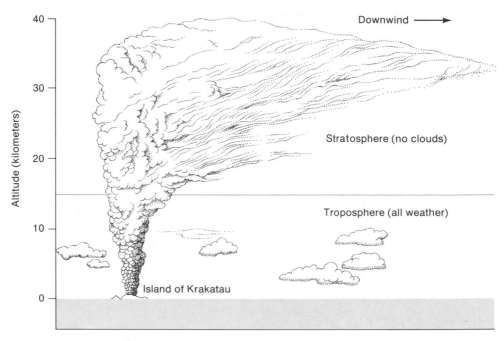

102 The Krakatau eruption cloud of 1883 was injected high into the stratosphere, where no rain clouds exist to wash the debris back to Earth. Once there, the fine dust stays in suspension for months to years. (After Richard Hazlett, 1978.)

aerosol layer changes over periods of months to years. It can increase suddenly with an injection of new aerosol from a volcanic eruption, but it takes several years to decrease to normal.

This layer of haze in the stratosphere apparently intercepts the incoming sunlight, heating the stratosphere and cooling the lower atmosphere as well as the Earth's surface. The 1963 eruption of Mount Agung volcano in Bali, Indonesia provided some of the first measurable evidence that this effect is real. The Balinese consider Agung to be the navel of the world, and they live with respect and reverence for this 3142 meter stratovolcano. After 120 years of repose Mount Agung began erupting on February 18, 1963. Major explosions produced destructive glowing avalanches on March 17 and May 16 which devastated many villages and killed 1900 people.

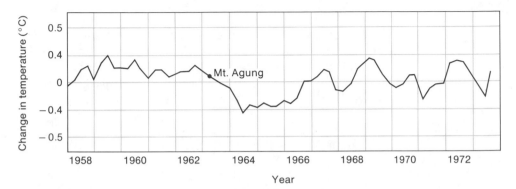

103 Graph of tropospheric temperatures shows world temperature disturbance apparently caused by the eruption of Agung Volcano in Bali, Indonesia in 1963. A lowering of average world temperatures by about 0.3 to 0.4 °C lasted 2 to 3 years. (After J. Hansen, W. Wang, and A. Lacis, *Science* 199, 1978, p. 1066. Copyright © 1978 by the American Association for the Advancement of Science.)

The explosion clouds of gas and volcanic dust reached heights of 10 kilometers above the crater, apparently high enough to inject volcanic debris into the stratosphere. The atmospheric effects, including fiery red sunsets and halos around the sun and moon, encircled the Earth within a few weeks; but the most convincing evidence was the decrease in starlight measured worldwide by astronomical observatories; the decrease was maximum from August to November 1963 and lasted until mid-1964. Measured stratospheric temperatures rose as much as 6°C, and the average world temperature dropped 0.5°C for three years after the eruption (Figure 103).

Although Agung was a major eruption, the explosion of Krakatau in 1883 was at least 10 times greater, both in terms of energy and the total volume of volcanic products. The key question, however, is how much volcanic dust and gas reached into the stratosphere from Agung as compared to Krakatau, and that is not known.

So the question remains: To what extent do volcanic eruptions affect our weather and climate? There will be no definite answer until scientists can determine the character and amount of volcanic debris that reaches the stratosphere, and measure its effects worldwide in terms of stratospheric heating and the cooling of the Earth's surface. That is a joint task for volcanologists and meteorologists. The project is of immense importance to a world that depends on a benign climate for its very existence.

15
Forecasting
Volcanic Eruptions

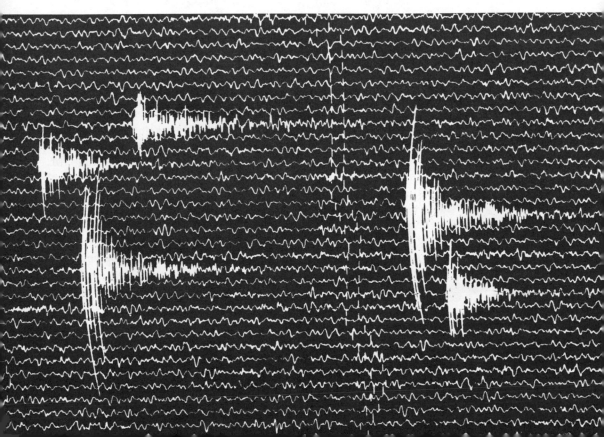

15 Forecasting Volcanic Eruptions

Nature cannot be commanded except by being obeyed.
Sir Francis Bacon (1561–1626)

Forecasting the time, place, and character of volcanic eruptions is one of the major goals in volcanology. We prefer the word forecast to prediction because the science of weather forecasting has established the concept that forecasts are probabilistic. That is, they are not precise; the hope is that they are more accurate than statistical averages.

For example, suppose that rainfall records in Hilo, Hawaii show that on the average it rains during 6 out of 10 days throughout the year. If a weatherman forecasts a 60 percent chance of rain tomorrow in Hilo he is not making a very adventurous statement. However, if the wind patterns and satellite photos indicate that chances are greater or less than average for rain tomorrow, then the forecast may say 90 percent chance of rain, or 10 percent chance of rain.

These would be valid forecasts based on information other than historical statistics; their worth can be evaluated in hindsight by comparison to random guesses. Weather forecasters avoid the word prediction because it sounds so precise and specific. Present weather forecasts, although far from 100 percent precise, are extremely valuable. They do much better than random guesses, and their batting average is improving.

The current goal in forecasting volcanic eruptions is to provide the best forecasts possible based on the statistical record of the volcano under study as well as on the day-to-day vital signs of the volcano in terms of earthquakes, surface deformation, temperature, gas emissions, and so forth.

The statistics of past eruptions are of great importance both as a basis for finding the average probability of eruption and as a means of deciphering some pattern in eruption habits. At least three patterns can be recognized even though the period of repose between eruptions varies from days to thousands of years.

One pattern is completely random. That is, no matter how long the repose period has been, the average chance for an eruption next month remains the same. This is like cutting cards to get an ace; no matter how many times you fail, the chance in the next cut is exactly the same: 4 out of 52. Mauna Loa Volcano in Hawaii appears to operate in this random manner; no matter how long or short the repose between eruptions, the average chance for a new eruption next month remains the same—2 percent.

Hekla Volcano in Iceland shows quite a different pattern of time intervals between eruptions. At Hekla the average probability of an eruption increases with time. This would be like cutting for aces and discarding the cut card each time you fail, thereby increasing the chance of getting an ace with each new cut.

Just the opposite occurs at volcanoes like Kilauea in Hawaii, where a group of eruptions will cluster together in time (Figure 104). In this situation the probability of an eruption decreases with time. There is no easy analogy for this in card-cutting.

Each of these time patterns in eruptive habit is important as a basis for forecasting future activity. Unfortunately, for the statistics to have any meaning, the number of eruptions (or cuts of aces) must exceed 10 or 20. Only a small fraction of the world's volcanoes are active enough or have been studied long enough to establish these patterns.

Dormant volcanoes are by no means dead, and by studying them with sensitive instruments it is possible to monitor their vital signs through periods of repose and awakening. The earthquake count is one of these vital signs.

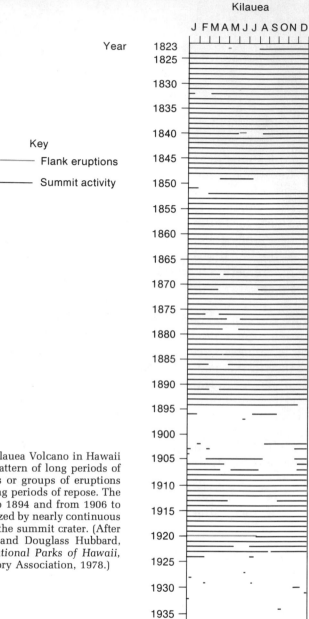

104 Eruptions of Kilauea Volcano in Hawaii since 1823 show a pattern of long periods of continuing eruptions or groups of eruptions interspersed with long periods of repose. The periods from 1823 to 1894 and from 1906 to 1924 were characterized by nearly continuous lava lake activity in the summit crater. (After Gordon Macdonald and Douglass Hubbard, *Volcanoes of the National Parks of Hawaii,* Hawaii Natural History Association, 1978.)

Year

Key
———— Flank eruptions
———— Summit activity

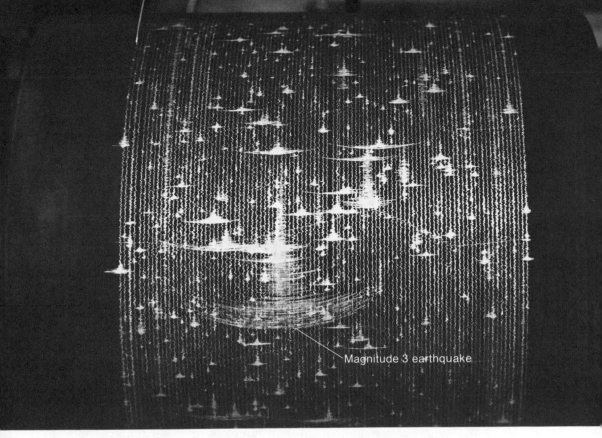

105 Seismograph recording earthquakes at the Hawaiian Volcano Observatory. The drum rotates once every 15 minutes, slowly enough that an entire day fits on one record sheet. Most of the microearthquakes on this record are too small to be felt. However the larger quake, whose seismogram is just to the left and below center, is about magnitude 3, large enough to be felt in a local area close to its source. (Photograph by the U.S. Geological Survey.)

Earthquakes and volcanoes both occur along plate margins, where most of the earthquakes are considered to be related to the slow grinding of the moving edges of the plates. However, some earthquakes appear to be more directly related to volcanic processes. In Hawaii and other areas of hot-spot volcanoes, earthquakes accompany volcanism even though the plate margins may be thousands of miles away. Several microearthquakes per day can almost always be recorded by sensitive seismographs on an active volcano, whether it is in eruption or not (Figure 105).

There is probably more than one cause for these volcanic earthquakes, including increasing topographic load, rapid underground temperature changes, moving magma, and gas explosions. The slipping and cracking of rocks underground to adjust to the growing weight of a huge volcano is only indirectly related to volcanic activity, but the other causes, particularly the movement of magma and the formation of cracks through which it can move, are closely connected to active volcanic processes.

Increases in the number or size of volcanic earthquakes, particularly those related to the conduits through which magma erupts to the surface, often occur before eruptions. However, the relationship is not infallible. In a study of 71 earthquake swarms and volcanic eruptions, 58 percent showed an increase in earthquake activity before eruptions, 38 percent showed an increase without eruptions, and in 4 percent there was an eruption without any increase in earthquake activity.

Because the background count of microearthquakes in volcanic areas is highly variable, only a large change in their number, by as much as a factor of 100, seems to be significant. Russian scientists in Kamchatka now think that large increases in the total energy released by volcanic earthquakes is more important than their increasing number. The time between the onset of increasing earthquakes and the actual eruption varies from weeks to hours, but even so, the number, size, and location of earthquakes on active volcanoes is an important index to forthcoming volcanic activity.

Volcanic tremor is a unique kind of seismic activity associated with volcanoes. It consists of more-or-less continuous ground vibration with a frequency of 0.5 to 10 cycles per second—a very low hum detectable by seismographs (Figure 106). Its source is not clear; various studies relate it to the formation of gas bubbles or the turbulent flow of magma, which creates a resonance like water hammering in poorly designed pipes. Whatever its source, it is nearly always present during volcanic eruptions, and often begins before the actual surface outbreak. However, not all periods of volcanic tremor are followed by eruptions. In Hawaii, high-amplitude volcanic tremor

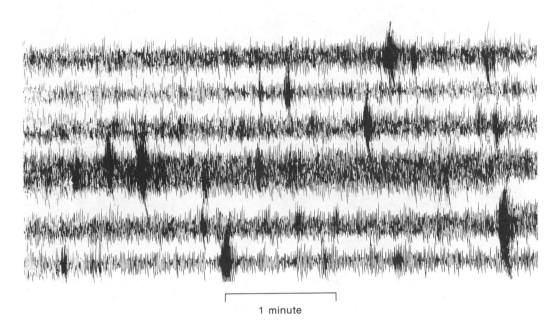

1 minute

106 Volcanic tremor recorded on a seismograph in Hawaii during the eruption of Kilauea in 1977. This low-frequency vibration of the ground at about 3 to 5 cycles per second is related to the movement of magma through underground conduits. The tremor starts before the breakout of eruptions and is a sign that an eruption is likely to occur. (Photograph by James Griggs, U.S. Geological Survey, 1977.)

is often the best indication that an eruption has begun or is about to begin within a few minutes or hours. A "tremor alarm" ringing in the houses of the Observatory staff brings them running regardless of the time of night.

Slight changes in the slopes or distances between survey points on the summits and flanks of active volcanoes provide another major method of diagnosing the internal changes taking place. Several techniques are involved, including conventional leveling and the determination of distances with reflected light beams (Figure 107). Tiltmeters, which can detect changes in slope smaller than 1 part per million, are also used. An angular change in slope of 1 part per million (1 microradian) is equivalent to lifting the end of a rigid board 1 kilometer long by only 1 millimeter (Figure 108).

107 Geodimeter being used to measure changes in distance related to volcanic deformation. The time it takes a laser beam to return from a reflector station accurately measures the distance between bench marks to a few millimeters. (Photograph by the U.S. Geological Survey.)

108 Tiltmeter in Hawaii. Brass pots filled with water and fastened to cement posts several meters apart are connected by hoses. Micrometers inside the pots allow the water levels to be read to a fraction of a millimeter. Tilting of the ground surface by as little as 1 part per million (a kilometer-long board lifted at one end by 1 millimeter) causes the water levels to change enough to be detected easily in these sensitive instruments. (Photograph by the U.S. Geological Survey.)

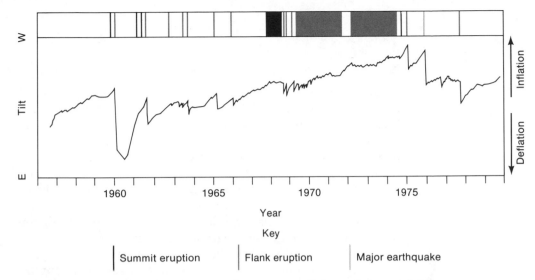

109 Twenty-year tilt record of Kilauea Volcano in Hawaii shows the ups and downs related to eruptions. For months to years before an eruption, the summit of Kilauea inflates. When it reaches a level that exceeds the strength of the rocks surrounding the shallow magma chamber, the volcano erupts. Some eruptions rapidly remove large volumes of magma from the summit chamber, and the volcano deflates over a period of days. A high level of inflation indicates a higher probability of eruption, but since the strength of the rocks surrounding the magma chamber varies from one eruption to another, no exact level of tilt can be used to predict the next eruption. (Data from the U.S. Geological Survey.)

Repeated at frequent intervals, these surveying techniques reveal the tiny, unseeable deformations of the volcano's surface caused by changes in magmatic pressure or volume inside the volcano. *Deformation monitoring,* the collective name for all of these individual surveying techniques, has become the second most important means of forecasting volcanic eruptions, preceded only by the monitoring of earthquakes.

The slow inflation of Kilauea Volcano in the months before an eruption, and the sudden collapse over a period of hours or days during an eruption (described in Chapter 6) has been revealed by deformation measurements in the past 20 years. The slow, more-or-less continuous addition of magma into the shallow chamber beneath Kilauea's summit causes the summit to swell upward as much as 2 meters over a diameter of 10 kilometers. This gentle bulge causes outward tilts and increasing distances between survey stations, similar to the changing relationship of spots on the surface of an inflating balloon (Figure 109).

Eruptions of Kilauea remove molten lava from the magma chamber faster than it is replenished, causing summit deflation, inward tilts, and contracting distances between survey stations. Deformation measurements provide a kind of magma barometer which in turn can be used to help forecast eruptions. If there were an exact level of inflation that triggered an eruption, the question of when an eruption will occur would be solved.

But nature is not that simple. On Kilauea, which has been tracked through more deformation cycles than any other single volcano, the degree of tilt at the Volcano Observatory just prior to the last 22 eruptions has always been relatively high, but has not shown any specific critical angle. Even so, the probability of an eruption increases with increasing inflation, so that the probability can be estimated as a percentage chance of eruption. For example, the average probability over the past 20 years of having an eruption begin during a one-week vacation in Hawaii is 2.4 percent. By examining the tilt graph of Kilauea over the past 20 years, you could have definitely improved on this statistical average. If the tilt was below 1100 microradians, no eruptions occurred; but above 1400 microradians of tilt, the chance that an eruption might begin during the following week increased to 10 percent.

Deformation measurements on several potentially explosive volcanoes of subducting plate margins are now under way, but it is not yet clear whether they will be as useful as those on basaltic shield volcanoes. One problem with explosive volcanoes is their long repose time between eruptions. It could take several hundred years to learn as much about the deformation at Vesuvius as has already been learned at Kilauea in the past 20 years.

Changes in the Earth's magnetic and electrical fields near volcanoes, which relate to the state of volcanic activity, have been observed in Japan, New Zealand, Kamchatka, and Hawaii. Although the techniques used for these observations are relatively new and not as well established as seismic and deformation measurements, their usefulness for forecasting eruptions looks promising.

Temperature changes at steam vents and warm springs on volcanoes would seem to be an obvious index for forecasting,

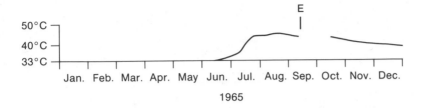

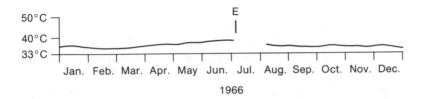

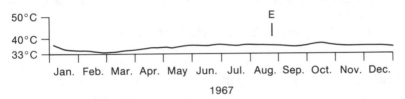

110 Changes in the temperature of the crater lake on Taal Volcano in the Philippines sometimes warn of forthcoming eruptions. In 1965 the temperature began to rise well above its background level of 33 °C in July; the volcano erupted in September. The 1966 eruption was preceded by a much less obvious temperature rise, and the 1967 eruption could not have been forecast on the basis of temperature alone. (Data from A. Alcaraz, Philippine Commission on Volcanology.)

but rainfall and changes in groundwater circulation often cause large fluctuations in temperature not related to volcanic activity. In one case, however, the 12 °C temperature rise of the crater lake at Taal Volcano in the Philippines clearly signaled its 1965 eruption (Figure 110).

Geochemical changes in the volume and composition of volcanic gases are also useful indicators of hidden changes beneath active volcanoes. New steam vents formed at Askja Volcano in Iceland two weeks before its 1961 eruption. Scientists in Japan, Kamchatka, and the United States have all reported an increase in sulfur gases (SO_2) relative to chloride gases (HCl) at volcanic steam vents in the years or days before an eruption.

Changes in the percentage of hydrogen, helium, and radon in volcanic gases are also under study as possible signals of changing volcanic activity.

No single technique appears to be the master key to forecasting volcanic eruptions. Each volcano is unique, and the case history of one cannot always be used to diagnose the symptoms of another. Even so, useful though not precise forecasting is currently being practiced on a few volcanoes in Japan, Indonesia, Iceland, the Philippines, Kamchatka, and Hawaii. Some recent notable successes and failures illustrate the present state of the art.

Mauna Loa erupted in July 1975 after 25 years of repose, its longest sleep in historic time. Deformation measurements on Mauna Loa had been started in 1965, but they showed little change until 1974 when the distance across the 3-kilometer-wide summit caldera increased by 75 millimeters. The number of earthquakes beneath Mauna Loa increased for more than a year before the eruption, and kept increasing up to the time of the eruption. Although the exact time of the eruption was not forecast, the awakening of Mauna Loa was well observed, and the public was informed of the increasing probability of an eruption. The short but intense summit eruption of 30 million cubic meters of lava on July 5 and 6, 1975 came as no surprise (Figure 111).

After the summit eruption of Mauna Loa, earthquakes and renewed inflation at the summit and along the northeast rift indicated that a flank eruption was imminent. Mauna Loa's pattern of summit eruptions followed by flank eruptions is evident from past records, and flank eruptions are more destructive since their flows often reach the cultivated and inhabited lower slopes of the Big Island. Northeast rift eruptions even threaten Hilo. An 1881 flow reached to within 2 kilometers of Hilo Harbor; some present suburbs of Hilo are built on this flow (Figure 112).

Scientists from the Hawaiian Volcano Observatory issued the warning that a flank eruption on the northeast rift of Mauna Loa was likely sometime before the summer of 1978. However,

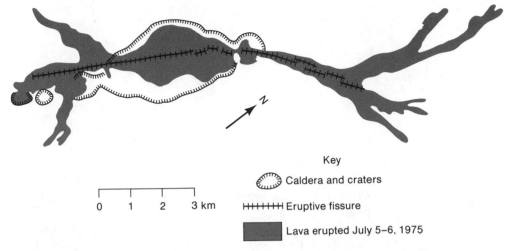

Key

 Caldera and craters

⊢+++++⊣ Eruptive fissure

Lava erupted July 5–6, 1975

111 Sketch map of the summit of Mauna Loa Volcano in Hawaii, showing the lavas erupted on July 5 and 6, 1975. The flows covered 13.5 square kilometers. With an average flow thickness of about 2.2 meters, they formed a volume of approximately 30 million cubic meters. (Data from *Bulletin of Volcanic Eruptions*, No. 15, 1977.)

112 Lava flows from the northeast rift of Mauna Loa Volcano in Hawaii have threatened the city of Hilo six times since 1850. The 1881 flow reached to within 2 kilometers of Hilo Harbor. Lava barriers to divert future flows from reaching Hilo were proposed in 1937, 1950, and 1979 but never built; their effectiveness remains unknown. (Map after Richard Hazlett, 1978.)

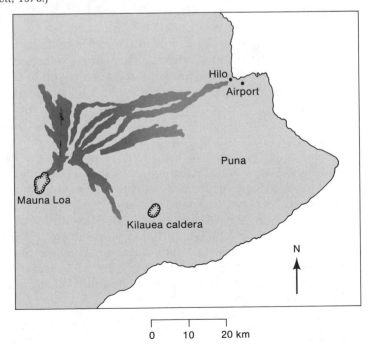

during 1977 the rate of inflation and number of earthquakes diminished rapidly and the forecast was retracted. Deflation of the summit has not occurred, and Mauna Loa may still be charged for another eruption.

Since detailed deformation and earthquake data for Mauna Loa have been kept only since 1974—through just part of an entire cycle between eruptions—it is not yet possible to interpret these data with any confidence. In forecasting the 1975 to 1978 activity of Mauna Loa, volcanologists can claim a .500 batting average; not bad, but far from precise.

The Russians may be doing better. The huge eruption of Tolbachik Volcano in Kamchatka in 1975 was preceded by a major earthquake swarm. Volcanologist P.I. Tokarev's published forecast that an eruption was imminent in the Tolbachik region during the next week allowed Russian television crews to be on hand for the birth of a new volcano on July 6, just two days after the forecast was issued (Figure 113).

However, real danger from volcanic hazards remains both a threat and a predicament to society. There are two La Soufrière Volcanoes in the Caribbean, one on the French island of Guadeloupe, the other on the British island of St. Vincent. In 1976, a small eruption of La Soufrière on Guadeloupe led to the massive and expensive evacuation of 74,000 residents because of the threat that the eruption might climax in catastrophic nuées ardentes similar to those of the Mont Pelée eruption on the neighboring island of Martinique in 1902. Fortunately, no major eruption took place; but unfortunately, volcanologists were blamed for their "cry wolf" forecast.

A new eruption in April 1979 at La Soufrière on St. Vincent posed the same problem. The initial explosions on St. Vincent were much more powerful than those on Guadeloupe, and many people evacuated by choice (Figure 114). Volcanologists and governing officials face a no-win situation. What does one cry out when there *may* be a wolf?

113 Great Tolbachik eruption in Kamchatka in 1975 was accurately forecast on the basis of increasing local earthquakes. The total volume of lava and pyroclastics erupted was nearly 2 cubic kilometers, and the ash cloud reached 14 kilometers high. (Photograph by N.P. Smelov, Institute of Volcanology, Kamchatka, U.S.S.R.)

114 Explosions and nuées ardentes occurred at La Soufrière Volcano on St. Vincent Island in the West Indies in April 1979. The evacuation of more than 17,000 inhabitants prevented a major disaster. The explosion shown here at dawn on April 22 has generated an ash cloud 6 kilometers high; it reached 14 kilometers several minutes later. (Photograph by Richard Fiske, Smithsonian Institution.)

The recent eruption of Mount St. Helens in the Cascade Range of the northwestern United States is a good example of where eruption forecasting now stands. In general, the forecasting was accurate and saved thousands of lives; in specific terms of the exact timing and magnitude of the eruption, it was not accurate enough.

Mount St. Helens had been known mainly for its serene beauty and its similarity in classic shape to Japan's Mount Fuji; it had not erupted since 1857. Until March 1980, the most recent eruption of a Cascade Volcano was that of Mt. Lassen in 1914. Both of these are subduction volcanoes, part of the Pacific's Ring of Fire, and thus are apt to erupt infrequently but explosively.

Based on the nature and sequence of prehistoric volcanic deposits on and near Mount St. Helens, Dwight Crandell and Donal Mullineaux of the U.S. Geological Survey had forecast in 1978 that St. Helens Volcano would probably erupt before the end of the twentieth century. On March 20, 1980 an earthquake swarm began beneath Mount St. Helens. The swarm increased on March 25, involving several earthquakes of magnitude 4 or greater per day. An eruption was anticipated, and small explosions from the summit began on March 27. Intermittent steam and ash eruptions on a small scale occurred from March 27 until April 21, and from May 7 until May 14, opening a crater on the snow- and ice-covered summit.

In mid-April, a more ominous sign was noted. Scientists comparing aerial photographs taken before and after the beginning of the activity noticed major deformation high on the north flank of the volcano. Careful measurement showed that the deformed area had bulged outward to the north by about 100 meters in the period before April 20. It continued to push out at an almost steady rate of 1.5 meters per day during late April and early May.

The small eruptions and major deformation were interpreted to indicate a shallow intrusion of magma into Mount St. Helens. Based on the severity of some prehistoric eruptions, the forest and the mountain resort region on the north flank of the volcano were evacuated.

115 Earthquakes started to shake Mount St. Helens in the northwestern United States on March 20, 1980. Small explosive eruptions began March 27. By April 10, the date of this view (looking north), a new summit crater was forming. (Photograph by Austin Post, U.S. Geological Survey.)

116 On May 18, 1980, a gigantic directed blast and avalanche destroyed the entire north flank of Mount St. Helens. The eruption cloud rose to 20 kilometers and covered large areas in eastern Washington, northern Idaho, and western Montana with fine ash up to 7 centimeters thick. The steam cloud in the background, left of the summit, formed where pyroclastic flows entered Spirit Lake. (Photograph looking northeast by Robert Krimmel, U.S. Geological Survey.)

On May 18 at 8:32 AM, a magnitude 5.1 earthquake triggered a gigantic volcanic explosion and avalanche that ripped apart the entire north flank of the cone with a directed blast of steam and rock that devastated over 400 square kilometers. A major avalanche of rock and ice fluidized by exploding steam raced down a valley for 24 kilometers, and tens of thousands of virgin Douglas Fir trees, 1 to 2 meters in diameter, were blown down for distances up to 20 kilometers. About 65 people were killed, including volcanologist Dave Johnston who was making deformation and gas measurements from an observation post 10 kilometers from the summit of Mount St. Helens.

The directed blast and avalanche were followed by a major 8-hour ash eruption accompanied by pyroclastic flows. The ash cloud reached over 20 kilometers in altitude, darkening the sky and depositing up to 7 centimeters of fine ash on eastern Washington. The original 2950-meter elevation of St. Helens was reduced to about 2550 meters and the entire north flank was blasted away, forming a giant amphitheater 1.5 kilometers wide and 3 kilometers long, open to the north. The floor of the newly formed crater is about 800 meters below the horseshoe-shaped crater rim on the east, south, and west. The volume of the ejected material was about 3 cubic kilometers.

In reviewing all the data prior to the sudden gigantic eruption—seismic, deformation, volcanic gases, and visual observations—there was no apparent evidence that the activity was about to take a tragic turn. The sudden change from small explosions to the giant blast was not foreseen. In the great eruption at Bezymianny in Kamchatka in 1956, which is thought to be the best analog for this type eruption, there was a period of a few months during which moderate explosions preceded the huge directed blast. A similar increase in eruptive energy was expected to precede any major eruption of Mount St. Helens. The scale of the May 18 eruption was also not anticipated. There are many more small eruptions than large ones recorded in prehistoric St. Helens deposits, and the scale of the directed blast deposits was unprecedented in its 30,000 year geologic history.

117 The huge explosive eruption of Mount St. Helens on May 18, 1980, reduced the original 2950-meter summit by nearly 500 meters, and formed this gigantic amphitheater 1.5 kilometers wide by 3 kilometers long, open to the north. Steam jets issue from the floor of the horseshoe-shaped crater. (Photograph looking south by Ross Hamilton, U.S. Geological Survey, May 30, 1980.)

The early evacuation of the mountain, a major recreation area just coming into the summer season, undoubtedly averted a major catastrophe; experts estimate that as many as 30,000 lives could have been lost. Most of those who died were in the warning area: those whose jobs included a calculated risk, like volcanologist Dave Johnston, two researchers and several loggers; homeowners who wouldn't leave their property; and volcano-watchers who had skirted the barriers and gone in on logging roads. Even so, if the magnitude of the eruption and its exact timing could have been forecast, those lives would also have been saved.

The study of volcanoes is a fledgling science. It has come a long way, but it has an even longer way to go on the path to a true understanding of volcanoes. This book is dedicated to those who will seek that path.

Glossary

aa A type of lava flow having a rough, fragmental surface.

active volcano A volcano that is erupting or has erupted in recorded history.

airfall deposit Pyroclastic fragments that have fallen from an eruption cloud.

andesite A volcanic rock type intermediate in composition between rhyolite and basalt.

angle of repose The steepest slope at which loose material will come to rest without slumping.

ash, volcanic Fine pyroclastic material, down to dust size, that is formed by explosive volcanic eruptions.

barograph An instrument that makes a continuous record of changes in atmospheric pressure.

basalt A dark, heavy lava rich in iron and magnesium and comparatively poor in silica; the common lava of Hawaii.

block, volcanic A solid fragment thrown out in an explosive eruption, ranging in size from about 6 centimeters to several meters in diameter.

bomb, volcanic A still-viscous lava lump thrown out in an explosive eruption, which takes on its rounded shape while in flight.

caldera A gigantic basin with steep walls at the summit of a volcano; larger than a crater.

cinder cone A steep conical hill formed by the accumulation of cinders and other loose material expelled from a volcanic vent by escaping gases.

cinder, volcanic A pyroclastic fragment of about 1 centimeter in diameter.

compressional margin The converging edges of two tectonic plates.

conduit The pipe or crack through which magma moves.

continental crust The solid outer layers of the Earth including granitic rocks on the continent.

continental drift The theory that horizontal movements of the Earth's surface cause slow relative movements of continents toward or away from one another.

crater A bowl- or funnel-shaped depression, generally in the top of a volcanic cone; often the major vent of volcanic products.

crystalline rock A hard rock composed of interlocking crystals; often of igneous origin.

dike A sheetlike body of intrusive igneous rock which cuts across the layering of the host rock.

dormant volcano A volcano that is not presently erupting but is considered likely to do so in the future.

dust, volcanic The finer particles of volcanic ash.

earthquake wave A general term for a vibrational wave produced by an earthquake.

effusive eruption An eruption consisting mainly of lava flows (as opposed to explosive eruption).

eruption cloud A gaseous cloud of volcanic ash and other pyroclastics that forms by volcanic explosion.

extinct volcano A volcano that is not erupting and is not expected to do so in the future; a dead volcano.

extensional margin The edges of tectonic plates that are moving apart.

fault A fracture in the Earth's crust along which there has been movement.

flank eruption Eruption from the side of a volcano (in contrast to a summit eruption).

fume A gaseous cloud without volcanic ash.

feldspar A light-colored mineral composed largely of silicon, oxygen, and aluminum.

geophysics The physical and mechanical aspects of geology (in contrast to geochemistry).

geothermal energy Energy derived from the internal heat of the Earth.

geothermal power Power generated by using the heat energy of the Earth.

granite A coarse-grained igneous rock composed mostly of quartz and feldspar.

heat transfer Movement of heat from one place to another.

hot-spot volcanoes Volcanoes related to a persistent heat source in the mantle.

hydrothermal reservoir An underground zone of porous rock containing hot water.

intrusion An igneous rock body formed when molten igneous rock forces its way into surrounding host rocks and then cools; also the process of forming such an igneous rock body.

island arc A curving chain of volcanic islands formed at a compressional plate boundary.

Kimberlite pipe A vertical pipe-shaped intrusion of unusual igneous rocks that often contain diamonds.

lava Magma or molten rock that has reached the surface; or its resulting solid rock after cooling.

lava dome A steep-sided, rounded extrusion of highly viscous lava, squeezed out from a volcanic vent.

lava lake A lake of molten lava in a volcanic crater or depression; refers to the solidified and partly solidified stages as well as to an active lava lake.

lava tube A hollow tunnel formed when the surface of a lava flow cools and solidifies and the still molten interior lava flowing through drains away.

linear vent A vent formed by a long fissure reaching the surface (in contrast to a single crater).

low-velocity layer The zone in the upper mantle, about 60 to 250 kilometers in depth, in which seismic velocities are lower than in the overlying layers.

magma Molten rock material with dissolved gases that forms igneous rocks on cooling; magma that reaches the surface is called lava.

magma chamber An underground reservoir in the Earth's crust filled with magma, from which volcanic materials are derived.

magmatic fluids Volcanic gases, especially water and carbon dioxide, dissolved in magma.

magnetic field A region in which magnetic forces exist.

mantle The zone of the Earth below the crust and above the core (to a depth of 3480 kilometers).

microearthquake An earthquake which is not felt but is detectable by a seismograph.

neck A vertical, pipelike intrusion that represents a former volcanic vent; usually used to describe an erosional remnant.

normal fault An inclined fault in which the lower block moves relatively downward.

nuée ardente A fast-moving, dense "glowing cloud" of hot volcanic ash and gas erupted from a volcano.

obsidian A black or dark-colored volcanic glass, usually composed of rhyolite.

oceanic crust The Earth's crust where it underlies the oceans, without the granite layer that forms continents.

olivine An olive-green mineral composed of iron, magnesium, silicon, and oxygen.

ore The naturally occurring material from which a mineral, or minerals, of commercial value can be extracted.

pahoehoe A type of lava flow with a smooth, billowy or undulating surface.

partial crystallization The stage of cooling of magma when it is partly solid crystals and partly liquid rock.

partial melt The stage of melting of rock when it is partly liquid rock and partly solid crystals.

pillow lava Interconnected, sacklike bodies of lava formed under water.

plate tectonics The theory that the Earth's crust is broken into about 10 large plates which slowly move about the surface.

plume A rising column of magma from deep in the mantle responsible for hot-spot volcanoes.

pluton A large igneous intrusion, formed at depth in the crust.

precipitate A solid forming from a solution.

pumice A form of volcanic glass so filled with gas bubble holes that it resembles a sponge and is very light.

pyroclastics Solid fragments formed by explosion or spraying from a volcanic vent; includes ash, cinders, and blocks.

quartz An important rock-forming mineral composed of silicon and oxygen (SiO_2).

ridge, oceanic A major submarine mountain range.

rift system The oceanic ridges, over 84,000 kilometers in length, formed where plates are separating and new crust is being created; also their on-land equivalents like the East African Rift.

Ring of Fire The regions of mountain-building earthquakes and volcanoes which surround the Pacific Ocean.

rhyolite A fine-grained volcanic rock with the same composition as granite; although rhyolite and granite have the same composition, they differ in texture.

seafloor spreading The mechanism by which new seafloor crust is created at oceanic ridges and slowly spreads away on the separating plates.

seamount An isolated tall mountain on the sea floor, generally volcanic.

sedimentary mud Loose fine-grained sediment with enough water to form soft mud.

seismic wave See earthquake wave.

seismograph An instrument that records the motions of the Earth's surface caused by seismic waves.

seismology The study of earthquakes, seismic waves, and the structure of the interior of the Earth.

shearing The motion of two surfaces sliding past one another.

shield volcano A gently sloping volcano in the shape of a flattened dome, built by flows of very fluid basaltic lava.

silica A chemical combination of silicon and oxygen.

silicate mineral A mineral largely composed of silicon and oxygen.

strato-volcano A steep volcanic cone built both by lava flows and pyroclastic eruptions.

stock A large igneous intrusion roughly circular in a horizontal plane.

strike-slip fault A nearly vertical fault with side-slipping displacement.

subduction zone The zone of convergence of two tectonic plates, one of which usually overrides the other.

tephra A general term for all airfall pyroclastics from a volcano.

thermal gradient The rate of change of temperature with distance or depth.

thrust fault A gently inclined fault whose upper side moves relatively upward.

tidal wave See tsunami.

transform fault A strike-slip fault connecting the offsets of mid-ocean ridges.

tsunami A great sea wave produced by a submarine earthquake or volcanic eruption.

vein A mineral deposit precipitated in a rock fracture.

vent The opening at the Earth's surface through which volcanic materials issue forth.

viscosity A measure of resistance to flow in a liquid; water has a low viscosity while honey has a high viscosity.

volcanic front The line of volcanoes closest to the oceanic trench in island arcs like Japan.

volcanic complex A persistent volcanic vent area that has built a complex mixture of volcanic landforms.

wave-cut terrace A level surface formed by wave erosion of coastal rocks; may appear above sea level if uplifted.

The World's 101 Most Notorious Volcanoes

Activity, size, shape, beauty, danger, location, and the authors' preferences were used to select the following list. More complete catalogs of active volcanoes from which much of the data in this appendix are derived are listed in the Bibliography.

ANTARCTICA

Deception Island A strato-volcano with a submarine caldera forming a horseshoe-shaped island. This snug harbor, protected from screaming antarctic storms, has recently been a base for various scientific expeditions. Small explosive eruptions interrupted expeditions' plans in 1967, 1969, and 1970.

Mount Erebus A snow-and-ice covered strato-volcano with an active lava lake in its summit crater. It was in eruption when first sighted in 1841 and has had several reported explosions since. The present lava lake, about 100 meters in diameter, apparently formed in the 1960s. Erebus is the world's farthest-south active volcano.

ATLANTIC OCEAN

Beerenberg A strato-volcano with a caldera, on Jan Mayen Island north of Iceland. It is the farthest-north active volcano, and has erupted 4 times since 1633. The last eruption was in 1970–1971.

Fayal A strato-volcano with a caldera and rift zones, in the Azores Islands. Explosive eruptions just offshore followed by lava flows in 1957–1958 added new land to the west cape of the island. Major lava flows from higher on the same rift zone occurred in 1672.

La Palma   A complex volcano with a caldera and rift zones, on the west end of the Canary Islands. Lava flows have erupted 6 times since 1585; the last time was in 1971.

CARIBBEAN SEA

Mont Pelée   A strato-volcano with summit domes. The explosive eruption on May 8, 1902 generated a nuée ardente which swept down the mountainside and within minutes incinerated the town of Saint-Pierre and its 28,000 inhabitants. Three other explosive eruptions have been recorded, the last in 1932. Photograph on page 66.

La Soufrière of Guadeloupe   A strato-volcano with a summit dome, on the southern part of Guadeloupe Island. It has erupted explosively about 10 times since 1400. The last eruption in 1976 prompted the evacuation of 70,000 people for several months, but turned out to be only minor explosions.

La Soufrière of St. Vincent   A strato-volcano with a crater lake. Its 7 eruptions since 1718 include two major explosive events. Evacuation in 1979 prevented a potential repeat of the tragedy of 1902 when 1600 deaths occurred, largely from nuées ardentes. Photograph on page 202.

CHILE

Calbuco   A strato-volcano in southern Chile. Lava flows and explosive eruptions from the snow- and ice-filled crater cause major mudflows and the destruction of arable lands. It has erupted 9 times since 1837, the last time in 1961.

Llullaillaco   A strato-volcano in northern Chile. This is the world's highest active volcano with a summit elevation of 6723 meters. Of the 3 recorded eruptions during the 1800s, two were explosive and the other a lava flow from a side vent. Nevado Ojos del Salado (6886 meters), also in Chile, is higher, but has only steam vents and no recorded eruptions.

Nilahue   A circular lake in Southern Chile formed by volcanic explosions. Eruptions in 1907 and 1955 formed 1-kilometer-wide lake basins in a valley between old volcanic cones. A 7-kilometer-high ash column in 1955 destroyed vegetation for a radius of 20 kilometers.

Villarrica A strato-volcano in central Chile. About 20 explosive eruptions and three lava flows have occurred since 1558. The eruption in 1971 melted large volumes of snow and ice, and the resulting mudflows killed 15 people. The last eruption was in 1980.

COLOMBIA

Puracé A complex strato-volcano in central Colombia. It has erupted explosively about 25 times since 1827, twice destroying arable land and causing deaths. The last eruption was in 1977.

COSTA RICA

Arenal A strato-volcano in northwestern Costa Rica. Dormant until 1968, it burst into eruption with a strong explosion throwing huge blocks as far as 5 kilometers; the explosion was followed by nuées ardentes. This initial eruption killed 78 people. Activity has continued since with the extrusion of thick, slow-moving lava flows.

Irazú A strato-volcano with a double crater, in central Costa Rica. It has erupted explosively about 15 times since 1723. The last major eruption lasted from 1963 until 1965; its numerous small to moderate ash falls were destructive to coffee plantations and a nuisance to the capital city of San Juan.

Poás A strato-volcano with twin crater lakes in central Costa Rica. It has erupted 19 times since 1834, generally with explosions of mud and water from the northern lake. The 1910 eruption shot a fountain of water more than 4 kilometers high. The last eruption was in 1979.

ECUADOR (ANDES MOUNTAINS)

Cotopaxi A strato-volcano nearly 6000 meters high. It has had over 50 eruptions since 1532 including major eruptions and lava flows. The 1877 eruption melted large volumes of snow and ice from the summit, causing mudflows that reached 100 kilometers down adjacent river beds. The last eruption was in 1942. Photographs on pages 117 and 119.

Guagua Pichincha   A strato-volcano with a caldera and a central cone. Although active from the 1500s to the 1800s, there have been no eruptions since 1881. Forty centimeters of ash from Guagua Pichincha fell on Quito in 1660; modern Quito climbs up the sides of this potentially dangerous volcano.

Reventador   A strato-volcano east of the main ranges of the Andes. Although this mysterious volcano was not explored until 1931, it was apparently the source of some ash falls in Quito as far back as 1541. An important oil pipeline connecting the Amazon fields to the west coast of Ecuador now crosses its north slope. The last eruption was in 1976.

ECUADOR (GALAPAGOS ISLANDS)

Fernandina   A shield volcano with a summit caldera. The most active of the Galapagos volcanoes, this uninhabited island was called Narborough in Darwin's chronicles. A major explosive eruption and 350-meter collapse of the caldera occurred in 1968. The last eruption was in 1978.

EL SALVADOR

Izalco   A young strato-volcano born in 1770 on the south flank of Santa Ana Volcano in western El Salvador. It had nearly continuous small explosive eruptions until 1957 and was known as the Lighthouse of the Pacific. When a hotel was built nearby to view the frequent eruptions, the activity stopped. The last eruption was in 1966.

ETHIOPIA

Erta Alè   A shield volcano with an active lava lake, in the rift valley of northern Ethiopia. Lava eruptions from fissures on the flank were observed in 1959–1960. The active lava lake discovered in 1967 has since been in constant eruption.

GREECE

Santorini   A strato-volcano with a submerged caldera, in the Aegean Sea. Its giant explosive eruption and caldera collapse in about

1500 B.C. buried Akroteri, an important Minoan city currently under excavation. The huge eruption and sudden sinking of the island's center beneath the sea may have been the source of the legend of Atlantis. The last eruption in 1950 formed a lava dome and thick lava flows on the islands within the caldera.

GUATEMALA

Atitlán A strato-volcano on the south rim of a 20-kilometer-diameter caldera lake in southwestern Guatemala. It has erupted with small to moderate explosions 11 times since 1469. The caldera lake, formed following immense prehistoric eruptions, is one of the most beautiful in the world.

Fuego A strato-volcano in southwestern Guatemala whose name means fire. It has erupted over 50 times since 1524, producing mostly explosions of ash but sometimes nuées ardentes and lava flows. The last eruption was in 1979.

Pacaya A volcanic complex of two small strato-volcano cones and older lava domes in Southern Guatemala. It has erupted over 20 times since 1565, generally with only explosions but with some lava flows in recent years. Eruptions have occurred nearly every year since 1965.

Santa Maria A strato-volcano with a growing lava dome on its southwest slope, in western Guatemala. Its first eruption in historic time was in 1902; it produced a giant explosion of 5.5 cubic kilometers of pumice fragments and ash. A lava dome named Santiaguito began growing in the explosion crater in 1922 and has since been erupting intermittently. The last eruption was in 1980.

ICELAND

Askja A complex volcano with a 10-kilometer-diameter caldera in central Iceland. Although most of its 8 eruptions since the fourteenth century have been lava flows, the great eruption of 1875 exploded 2 cubic kilometers of ash over much of eastern Iceland. The resulting near-famine led many Icelanders to emigrate to the United States and Canada. The last eruption was in 1961.

Grímsvötn A caldera in the Vatnajökull Icecap of south-central Iceland. It has erupted beneath the ice about 25 times since 1332, causing gigantic floods called glacial bursts. The sudden floods often exceed the flow volume of the Amazon River.

Heimaey A cinder cone with a thick blocky lava flow from its north side, in the Vestmann Islands off the south coast of Iceland. A 2-kilometer-long fissure opened near the fishing port of Heimaey in 1973. Cinders and ash soon covered much of the evacuated town of 5000 inhabitants, and the thick flow nearly closed off the harbor entrance. The courageous Icelanders returned to a better harbor, rebuilt their town, and even heat their hospital with steam from the cooling flows.

Hekla A strato-volcano elongated by a northeast-trending rift system in south-central Iceland. It has erupted about 20 times since the settling of Iceland in 900 A.D., generally with ash explosions followed by lava flows. In Medieval Europe, Hekla was considered the gate to Hell. The last eruption was in 1980.

Krafla A complex volcano with a large central caldera, in northern Iceland. Dormant after a series of eruptions in 1724–1728, Krafla awakened in 1975 with small eruptions and episodes of extensive ground cracking. The eruption in 1977 also sprayed a small amount of lava out of a producing geothermal steam well, the only known case of an eruption from a man-made vent. Photographs on pages 39 and 41.

Laki A fissure zone over 25 kilometers long, in south-central Iceland. Its single giant eruption in 1783 produced over 12 cubic kilometers of lava, a historic record, filling two river valleys and covering more than 500 square kilometers. Stunted grass and fluorine poisoning from the accompanying volcanic gases starved and killed most of Iceland's livestock. The ensuing famine caused 10,000 deaths. Photograph on page 179; map on page 111.

Surtsey A cinder-cone and lava-flow island on the south coast of Iceland. Born from the sea in 1963 and erupting until 1967, it has provided scientists a view of how new land forms and how plants and animals establish themselves in this new territory. Chapter 2 has photographs and additional information on Surtsey.

INDIAN OCEAN

Karthala A shield volcano with a summit caldera, on the southern part of Grand Comoro Island. It has erupted about 20 times since 1828, mainly lava flows that issue from the summit or rift zones. The last eruption was in 1977.

Piton de la Fournaise A shield volcano with a caldera, on the eastern part of Reunion Island. Sometimes called a sister to Hawaiian volcanoes because of the similarity of climate and volcanic nature, it has erupted lava flows over 100 times since 1640. The last eruption was in 1979.

INDONESIA

Agung A strato-volcano in Bali considered in legend to be the navel of the world. Although it has erupted explosively only 4 times since 1808, the last eruption in 1963–1964 was of major proportions. High ash explosions affected world climate and nuées ardentes killed many people.

Dieng A complex volcanic plateau with 26 cones and craters in central Java. It has erupted about 10 times since 1825. The last eruption in 1979 consisted of poisonous gases that killed 150 people.

Galunggung A strato-volcano with a lava dome, in western Java. It has erupted only 3 times in history, but the first in 1822 produced a 22-kilometer-long mudflow that killed 4000 people. The last eruption was in 1918.

Kawah Idjen A strato-volcano with a crater lake on the rim of a large caldera, in eastern Java. Although it has erupted 6 times since 1796, taking lives in 1817, it is most famous for its 1-kilometer-diameter lake of hot acid water. The last eruption was in 1958.

Kelut A strato-volcano with a crater lake, in eastern Java. It has erupted 30 times since about 1000 A.D. The explosive eruptions eject the hot crater lake and cause widespread destruction. In the 1919 eruption, over 100 villages were destroyed or damaged by mudflows that killed 5100 people. The last eruption was in 1967.

Krakatau Strato-volcano islands around a submerged caldera, in the Sunda Strait between Sumatra and Java. The 1883 eruption was one of the largest natural explosions in recorded time. Sounds were heard for 4000 kilometers, the emitted ash and pumice blocks totaled 18 cubic kilometers, the 6-kilometer-diameter caldera collapsed, and the resulting tsunami killed 36,000 people on the low shores of Java and Sumatra. The last eruption was in 1980. Chapter 4 has photographs and a detailed description.

Merapi A strato-volcano with a summit lava dome in central Java whose name means mountain of fire. It has erupted over 60 times since 1006 A.D., generally with explosions and nuées ardentes. The 1006 eruption caused so much death and destruction that the Hindu Rajah moved to Bali, and Mohammedanism took over Java. The last eruption was in 1980.

Papandajan A complex strato-volcano in western Java. Although it has had only 2 historic eruptions, the explosions and landslides in 1772 destroyed 40 villages and killed 3000 people. The last eruption was in 1925.

Peak of Ternate A strato-volcano island with multiple craters and crater lakes, west of Halmahera. It has erupted explosively over 60 times since 1538, sometimes producing lava flows. The last eruption was in 1963.

Semeru A strato-volcano with a summit lava dome, in eastern Java. Its nearly 70 eruptions, generally explosions which are sometimes accompanied by nuées ardentes and lava flows, make it one of Java's most active as well as its highest (3620 meters) volcano. The last eruption was in 1980.

Tambora A strato-volcano with a summit caldera, on Sumbawa Island. Its giant eruption in 1815 may have exceeded the size and power of Krakatau. The explosion, followed by caldera collapse, is estimated to have produced between 30 and 150 cubic kilometers of ash and blocks. Ten thousand people were killed by the eruption and 80,000 starved in the resulting crop loss and famine. World climate may have been affected. The last eruption was before 1913.

ITALY

Etna A transitional shield-to-strato-volcano in northeastern Sicily. It has erupted lava flows over 150 times since activity was first recorded in 1500 B.C. Small to moderate explosive eruptions occur at the summit; one in 1979 took 9 lives.

Monte Nuovo A cinder cone west of Naples with a small crater lake. This new mountain, about 1 kilometer in diameter and 100 meters high was born and built in the year 1538, most of it in the first few days of eruption. It has been dormant since its violent birth.

Stromboli A strato-volcano island west of Italy. Known as the Lighthouse of the Mediterranean, it has been in almost continuous eruption for over 2000 years. Small explosions of incandescent lava hurled up from the crater every 15 to 30 minutes are visible to ships passing by. Larger eruptions, some with lava flows, take place every several years.

Vesuvius A complex strato-volcano east of Naples. Most famous for its 79 A.D. eruption that buried Pompeii, it has since erupted over 50 times. Explosive eruptions are generally followed by lava flows. The last eruption was in 1944. Photographs on pages 34 and 177.

Vulcano A strato-volcano west of Italy. Legendary forge of Vulcan, this small island has provided the family name for all volcanoes. It has erupted explosively about 10 times since 200 B.C., the last time in 1888.

JAPAN

Asama A complex strato-volcano in central Japan. It has erupted over 100 times since 685 A.D., generally with a series of small explosions. In 1783 large nuées ardentes and resulting mudflows buried villages, killing 1300 people. Scientists at the Asama Volcano Observatory, started in 1909, have found earthquake counts and locations to be useful in forecasting eruptions.

Aso A group of cinder cones and small strato-volcanoes within a 20-kilometer-diameter caldera. One vent has erupted over 100 times since 796 A.D., generally as single, isolated explosions. Tourists visiting the rim of the active vent are sometimes killed by the ejected blocks and bombs. This last occurred in 1979.

Bandai A strato-volcano with a caldera, in north-central Japan. It has erupted 6 times since 806 A.D., including the major explosions which formed the caldera in 1888. The debris from this explosive excavation, amounting to 1.2 cubic kilometers, swept down the north flank of Bandai burying villages and killing 460 people.

Bayonnaise Rocks Lava domes sometimes building ephemeral islands inside a submarine caldera southeast of Japan. This submarine volcanic center has erupted over 10 times since it was first witnessed in 1896, sometimes building an island up to 95 meters high. A Japanese oceanographic ship investigating the area was destroyed by an explosion in 1952 with the loss of all 31 persons on board. The last eruption was in 1970.

Fuji A classic strato-volcano in central Japan, the archetype of volcanic form. It has erupted ash and lava about 15 times since 781 A.D. The last eruption in 1707 was from a vent high on the southeast side which ejected 0.8 cubic kilometer of ash, blocks, and bombs. The finer ash reached Tokyo. Picture on page 65.

Oshima A strato-volcano island with a caldera and a central cone, off the east coast of Central Japan. It has erupted about 50 times since 684 A.D., sometimes explosively and sometimes with extensive lava flows. The last eruption was in 1974.

Sakura-zima A strato-volcano forming a peninsula into Kagosima Bay, southern Japan. One of the world's most active volcanoes, it has had thousands of small explosive eruptions since the first recorded one in 708 A.D. Many deaths occurred in 1476 and 1779, but sufficient warning from earthquakes kept the death toll to only a few persons in the giant eruption of 1914 which produced

0.6 cubic kilometer of ash and 1.6 cubic kilometers of thick lava flows. The last eruption was in 1980.

Tarumai A complex strato-volcano with a lava dome, in northern Japan. It has erupted explosively about 35 times since 1667. A major eruption in 1909 discharged large volumes of ash and bombs, and was followed by the growth of the lava dome. The last eruption was in 1979.

Unzen Multiple lava domes form this complex volcanic peninsula on the west coast of southern Japan. Although only 5 eruptions have been recorded since 860, the 1792 activity involved either an explosion or earthquake which triggered a 0.5-cubic-kilometer avalanche. The slide and resulting tsunami caused 14,000 deaths.

Usu A strato-volcano with summit and flank lava domes, in northern Japan. Although it has erupted only 7 times since 1663, most of these eruptions have been explosive and destructive to life or land. In 1910, 1943–1944, and 1977–1979, large lava domes or ground surface uplifts, kilometers in diameter and tens to hundreds of meters high, were slowly forced upward.

MEXICO

Colima A strato-volcano with a summit lava dome, in west-central Mexico. Its 15 eruptions since 1576 have been mostly explosive with some lava flows. The last eruption was in 1976.

Paricutin A cinder cone in central Mexico. Born in a cornfield in 1943, it built a 410-meter-high cone with extensive lava fields during its brief lifespan. Most of the 1.3 cubic kilometers of ash and cinders, and much of the 0.7 cubic kilometer of lava were produced in the first few years. The eruption ended in 1952.

Popocatépetl A snow-capped strato-volcano dominating the skyline south of Mexico City. It erupted with small explosions 11 times between 1512 and 1697. Since a major explosion in 1720 only 3 small eruptions have occurred, the last in 1943.

NEW GUINEA

Karkar A strato-volcano island with a summit caldera, off the north coast of New Guinea. It has erupted about 10 times since 1643. The eruption in 1979 took the lives of volcanologists Robin Cooke and Elias Ravian.

Lamington A strato-volcano with a lava dome, in Papua (eastern New Guinea). This dormant volcano suddenly exploded in 1951. The nuées ardentes devastated over 200 square kilometers and killed about 3000 people. A 500-meter-high lava dome grew in the explosion crater from 1951 to 1956. The volcano has been quiet since then.

Rabaul A group of small volcanoes around the rim of a caldera bay on New Britain Island. Although the vents around Rabaul Harbour have erupted only 6 times since 1767, the violent explosive eruption in 1937 formed Vulcan crater, generated tsunamis, and killed 500 people. The last eruption was in 1943.

NEW ZEALAND

Ngauruhoe A strato-volcano with a near perfect cone in central North Island. It has had over 50 explosive eruptions since 1839, some with small nuées ardentes. The latest eruption was in 1975. Photograph on page 130.

Ruapehu A strato-volcano with a hot crater lake. There have been over 30 small explosions of steam and ash from the crater lake since 1861. Mudflows from the erupting lake occasionally flood adjacent valleys. One such flow on Christmas Eve in 1953 swept away a railroad bridge, wrecking the Wellington-Auckland Express and causing 151 deaths. The latest eruption was in 1980. Photograph on page 130.

Tarawera A volcanic complex of rhyolite domes in central North Island. A great eruption along a 17-kilometer-long fissure in 1886 ejected 1.3 cubic kilometers of basaltic ash and hot mud. The eruption occurred during one night, burying three villages and killing over 150 persons. From 1900 to 1904 Waimangu (black water) Geyser erupted in one of the craters formed along the 1886 fissure. Occasional geyser bursts of 400 to 500 meters during that time were the highest ever recorded.

White Island A strato-volcano in the Bay of Plenty north of New Zealand, with a large horseshoe-shaped crater. About 30 small to moderate explosive eruptions have occurred since 1826. Eleven men were killed and a sulfur works destroyed in the 1914 eruption and landslide. The last eruption was in 1980.

NICARAGUA

Cerro Negro A cinder cone in western Nicaragua whose name means black hill. Born in 1850, it has erupted about 15 times in its brief life span. Explosive eruptions from the central crater are often accompanied by lava flows that issue from near the base of the cinder cone. The last eruption was in 1971. Photograph on page 57.

Coseguina A strato-volcano with a central caldera lake, in western Nicaragua. A single major explosive eruption occurred in 1835 that scattered ash throughout Central America and southern Mexico. The ash cloud blotted out the sun over an area 300 kilometers wide.

Masaya A caldera with small central strato-volcanoes in southwestern Nicaragua. It has erupted nearly 20 times since 1524 with varied activity including explosions, lava flows, and lava lakes. The last eruption was in 1978. Photograph on page 124.

PACIFIC OCEAN

Ambrym A strato-volcano within a huge caldera in the New Hebrides Islands. Although the record is incomplete, it has been very active with many ash explosions and lava flows since its discovery in 1774. The last eruption was in 1979.

Falcon A submarine volcano in the Tonga Islands, famous for its appearing and disappearing islands. Cinder-cone islands formed during eruptions in 1885 and 1927 have been washed away by the sea into shallow banks. An island formed from 1927 to 1933 grew to 3 kilometers in diameter and 150 meters in height. The last eruption was in 1970.

Niuafo'ou A shield volcano with a central caldera and crater lake. This nearly perfect ring-shaped island in the Tonga group has had 10 eruptions since 1814, mostly small explosions with lava flows. The last eruption was in 1946.

Raoul A complex strato-volcano island with a caldera and crater lakes, in the Kermadec Islands north of New Zealand. This remote volcano is noteworthy because a research seismic station there, part of a worldwide net, gave warning of the 1964 eruption by recording a forerunning swarm of local earthquakes.

Rumble III A submarine volcano between New Zealand and the Kermadec Islands. Detected by underwater noises on hydrophones, this active seamount rises to within 120 meters of the sea surface. At least 4 eruptions were heard but not seen between 1958 and 1970.

Yasour A strato-volcano in the New Hebrides Islands. It has been in almost constant mild eruption since its discovery in 1774. Numerous small explosions hurl lava bombs 20 to 200 meters in the air.

PERU

El Misti A classic strato-volcano rising high above the city of Arequipa. Small explosive eruptions, the last in 1870, and gentle steaming characterize its historic activity. It is noted for its beauty rather than its habits.

PHILIPPINES

Mayon A classic strato-volcano cone in the central Philippines. It has erupted explosively over 40 times since 1616, often producing nuées ardentes and lava flows. The region is densely populated and at least eight eruptions have killed people. The last eruption was in 1978. Photograph on page 122.

Taal A strato-volcano island within a huge caldera lake in the central Philippines. It has erupted over 30 times since 1572, generally explosions which are sometimes accompanied by tsunamis in the lake. This killer volcano took many lives in 1716, 1749, 1754, 1874, 1911, and 1965. The last eruption was in 1977.

TANZANIA

Ol Doinyo Lengai A strato-volcano in northern Tanzania whose name means Mountain of God. Although it has erupted over 10 times since 1880, this volcano is more famous to science for its unusual lava flows composed in part of sodium carbonate (washing soda). The last eruption was in 1967. Photograph on page 175.

UNION OF SOVIET SOCIALIST REPUBLICS (KAMCHATKA)

Bezymianny A complex strato-volcano in central Kamchatka. Small explosive eruptions beginning in 1955 climaxed in a gigantic explosion in 1956, forming a mushroom cloud 35 kilometers high (photograph on page 67.) The thick, hot ash-flow deposits formed the Valley of Ten Thousand Smokes of Kamchatka, a feature similar to that created by the Katmai eruption in Alaska in 1912. The last eruption was in 1979.

Karymsky A strato-volcano within an ancient caldera in southeast Kamchatka. Its nearly 35 eruptions since 1771 have been mostly explosive. The last eruption was in 1976.

Kliuchevskoi A classic strato-volcano in central Kamchatka. It has erupted explosively over 70 times since 1697, often producing lava flows. The last eruption was in 1980.

Tolbachik A strato-volcano with a caldera, in central Kamchatka. After about 20 moderate eruptions since 1740, it produced a giant fissure eruption in 1975 that built several large cinder cones and major lava flows totaling nearly 2 cubic kilometers in volume. Forerunning earthquake swarms led to a prediction of the time and place of the 1975 eruption, precise enough that TV camera crews were on location for the outbreak. Photograph on page 201.

UNITED STATES (ALASKA)

Augustine A strato-volcano island with a summit lava dome, in the Cook Inlet, southern Alaska. It has erupted explosively 6 times since 1812. Dangers from major ash falls or volcanically generated tsunamis worry the offshore oil developers located nearby. The last eruption was in 1976.

Bogoslof A submarine volcano producing ephemeral lava domes in the central Aleutian Islands. It has erupted about 10 times since 1796, and in 1887 formed an island 160 meters high. Explosions and storm waves demolish the islands a few years after their birth. The last eruption was in 1931.

Katmai A complex strato-volcano with a summit caldera and lake, on the Alaska Peninsula. The 1912 eruption of Katmai was among the world's largest in historic time. In 2 days thick ash deposits covered a huge area, and a glowing avalanche filled a valley 3 kilometers wide and 20 kilometers long creating the Valley of Ten Thousand Smokes. The summit caldera, 3 kilometers in diameter, formed by collapse during the eruption. The total volume of the ash and glowing avalanche was 25 cubic kilometers. Although most of the valley "smokes" (steam vents) are now dead, Mount Trident, a new vent on the west flank of Katmai, became active in 1949 and has exploded and extruded thick lava flows several times. The last eruption of Trident was in 1974.

Shishaldin A classic strato-volcano cone in the eastern Aleutian Islands. It has a record of about 30 small to moderate explosive eruptions since 1775. Its sharp, snow-covered peak often has a plume of volcanic gases. The last eruption was in 1979.

UNITED STATES (CASCADE RANGE)

Lassen Peak A strato-volcano with a summit lava dome, in Northern California. It had a series of explosive eruptions in 1914–1915 which culminated in hot avalanches in May 1915. Small explosions occurred again in 1917. Photograph on page 123.

Mount Baker A snow and ice covered strato-volcano in northern Washington. Small explosive eruptions were reported in 1843, 1854, 1858, 1859, and 1870. Dormant since then, it began steaming in 1975 and has stayed in this state of mild activity to the present time.

Mount Rainier A massive, glacier-covered strato-volcano near Seattle, Washington. It has been dormant since about 1850 when a small explosive eruption apparently occurred. Small steam vents issue from the edges of the snow-and-ice-filled summit crater. Photographs on pages 131 and 133.

Mount St. Helens A snow-covered strato-volcano in southern Washington known for its beauty and serenity before its gigantic explosive eruption on May 18, 1980. A directed blast leveled 400 square kilometers of forest, and a major debris flow filled a valley for 24 kilometers. The 2950-meter-high summit was lowered by 400 meters, forming a deep horseshoe crater facing north. About 65 people were killed, including David Johnston, a volcanologist. Photographs on frontispiece and pages 204, 205, and 207.

UNITED STATES (HAWAII)

Kilauea A shield volcano with a summit caldera, on the Island of Hawaii. Famous for its active lava lake during the 1800s and early 1900s, it has also erupted extensive lava flows more than 50 times from both the summit and rift zones. The last eruption was in 1979. Chapter 6 has photographs and additional information.

Mauna Loa A massive shield volcano with a summit caldera, on the Island of Hawaii. It has erupted large lava flows from both the summit and rift zones 37 times since 1832, producing a total of nearly 4 cubic kilometers of basalt. The last eruption was in 1975. Photograph on page 128; maps on page 199.

ZAIRE

Nyamuragira A shield volcano with a summit caldera, in eastern Zaire. It has erupted over 20 times since 1894, including lava lake activity during 1921 to 1938. The last eruption was in 1980.

Nyiragongo A strato-volcano with a summit caldera, in eastern Zaire. It has erupted about 15 times since 1884, including lava lake activity from 1935 to 1977. A major fissure eruption on the south flank in 1977 drained the lava lake and rapidly covered an area of several square kilometers with very fluid lavas. About 300 people were killed by these flows.

Volcano Information Centers of the World

Volcanoes change, and so do the people and institutions who study them. The information centers listed in this appendix are those whose staffs have a major interest in active volcanism. The list is probably not complete, but it does provide contacts for obtaining data on active volcanoes in most areas of the world.

AZORES

Department of Geology
Azores University
Horta, Azores

CHILE

Departamento de Geologia
Universidad de Chile
Casilla 7556 Correo 3
Santiago, Chile

Universidad del Norte
Casilla 1280
Antofagasta, Chile

COLOMBIA

Instituto Geofisico
Apartado Aéreo 5315
Bogotá, Colombia

COSTA RICA

Instituto de Volcanologia
Universidad Nacional
Heredia, Costa Rica

ECUADOR

Charles Darwin Research Station
Galapagos Islands
Ecuador

Departamento de Geologia
Escuela Politecnica Nacional
Casilla 2759
Quito, Ecuador

EL SALVADOR

Centro de Investigaciones Geotécnicas
Apartado 06-109
San Salvador, El Salvador

ENGLAND

British Museum
Cromwell Road
London SW 7 5BD, England

Department of Geology
Imperial College
Royal School of Mines
Prince Consort Road
London SW 7 2BP, England

Institute of Geological Sciences
154 Clerkenwell Road
London EC 1R 5DU, England

ETHIOPIA

Geophysical Observatory
University of Addis Ababa
P.O. Box 1176
Addis Ababa, Ethiopia

FRANCE

Equipé Vulcain
B.P. 5
68700 Cernay, France

Institut de Physique du Globe de Paris
Tour 14, 4, place Jussieu
75230 Paris, France

Laboratoire de Volcanologie
C.F.R. (C.N.R.S.)
91190 Gif-sur-Yvette, France

GERMANY

Institut fur Mineralogie
Ruhr-Universitat
Postfach 102148
D-4630 Bochum 1, Germany

Mineralogisches Institut
Universitat
Albertstrasse 23b
D-7800 Freiburg, Germany

Mineralogisch-Petrographisches Institut
Universitat Tübingen
Wilhelmstrasse 56
D-74 Tübingen, Germany

GUATEMALA

Instituto Geografico Nacional
Zona 13
Ciudad de Guatemala, Guatemala

ICELAND

Nordic Volcanological Institute
University of Iceland
Reykjavík, Iceland

JAPAN

Departments of Geology and Geophysics
Hokkaido University
Sapporo, 060, Japan

Department of Geophysics
Kyoto University
Uji, Kyoto 611, Japan

Earthquake Research Institute
University of Tokyo
Bunkyo-ku
Tokyo 113, Japan

Seismological Division
Japan Meteorological Agency
1-3-4 Otemachi, Chiyoda-ku
Tokyo 100, Japan

INDONESIA

Volcanological Survey of Indonesia
Diponegoro 57
Bandung, Indonesia

ITALY

Centro di Studio per la Geologia Tecnica
Via Eudossiana 18
Roma, Italy

Istituto de Vulcanologia
Corso Italia, 55
95129 Catania, Italy

Istituto Internazionale de Vulcanologia
Viale Regina Margherita 6
95123 Catania, Italy

Osservatorio Vesuviano
8 0056 Resina
Napoli, Italy

MEXICO

Instituto de Geofisica
Universidad de Mexico
Mexico 20, D.F., Mexico

NEW HEBRIDES

Geological Survey Department
British Residency
Vila, New Hebrides

NEW ZEALAND
Geology Department
Victoria University
Private Bag
Wellington, New Zealand

New Zealand Geological Survey
P.O. Box 499
Rotorua, New Zealand

NICARAGUA
Instituto de Investigaciones Sismicas
Apartado 1761
Managua, Nicaragua

PAPUA NEW GUINEA
Volcanological Observatory
Geological Survey of Papua New Guinea
P.O. Box 386
Rabaul, Papua New Guinea

PERU
Departamento de Geologia
Universidad Nacional de San Augustin
Calle San Camilo 303A
Arequipa, Peru

PHILIPPINES
Commission on Volcanology
5th Floor, Hizon Building
Quezon Avenue
Quezon City, Philippines

RÉUNION ISLAND
Laboratoire de Géologie
Centre Universitaire de la Réunion
Réunion Island

SOLOMON ISLANDS
Geological Survey
G.P.O. Box G 24
Honiara, Solomon Islands

SPAIN
Departamento de Petrologia y Geochimica
Ciudad Universitaria
Madrid 3, Spain

UNION OF SOVIET SOCIALIST REPUBLICS
Institute of Volcanology
Piip Avenue, 9 Petropavlovsk
Kamchatsky, 683006, USSR

World Data Center B1
Molodezhnaya 3
Moscow 117 296, USSR

UNITED STATES
Geophysical Institute
University of Alaska
Fairbanks, Alaska 99701

Hawaiian Volcano Observatory
Hawaii National Park
Hawaii 96718

Office of Geochemistry and Geophysics
U.S. Geological Survey
Reston, Virginia 22092

Scientific Event Alert Network
Smithsonian Institution
Washington, D.C. 20560

World Data Center A for Solid-Earth
Geophysics, Environmental Data
and Information Service, NOAA
Boulder, Colorado 80303

WEST INDIES
Seismic Research Unit
University of the West Indies
St. Augustine
Trinidad, West Indies

ZAIRE
Department of Seismology
I.R.S.
Lwiro, D/S Bukavu (Kivu)
Zaire

APPENDIX C

Metric–English conversion table

Length	
1 centimeter	0.3937 inch
1 inch	2.5400 centimeters
1 meter	3.2808 feet
1 foot	0.3048 meter
1 meter	1.0936 yards
1 yard	0.9144 meter
1 kilometer	0.6214 mile
1 kilometer	3281 feet
1 mile	1.6093 kilometers

Area	
1 square centimeter	0.1550 square inch
1 square inch	6.452 square centimeters
1 square meter	10.764 square feet
1 square meter	1.1960 square yards
1 square foot	0.0929 square meter
1 square kilometer	0.3861 square mile
1 square mile	2.590 square kilometers

Volume	
1 cubic centimeter	0.0610 cubic inch
1 cubic inch	16.3872 cubic centimeters
1 cubic meter	35.314 cubic feet
1 cubic foot	0.02832 cubic meter
1 cubic meter	1.3079 cubic yards
1 cubic yard	0.7646 cubic meter

Mass	
1 gram	0.03527 ounce
1 ounce	28.3495 grams
1 kilogram	2.20462 pounds
1 pound	0.45359 kilogram

Density	
1 gram/cubic centimeter	62.4280 pounds/cubic foot

Pressure	
1 kilogram/square centimeter	0.96784 atmosphere
1 kilogram/square centimeter	0.98067 bar
1 kilogram/square centimeter	14.2233 pounds/square inch
1 bar	0.98692 atmosphere
1 atmosphere	1.0332 kilogram/square centimeter

Temperature	
(Celsius $\times \frac{9}{5}$) + 32	Fahrenheit
(Fahrenheit − 32) $\times \frac{5}{9}$	Celsius

Energy	
1 erg	2.39006×10^{-8} gram calorie
1 joule	10^7 ergs
Explosion equivalent to 1000 tons of TNT	4×10^{19} ergs

Power	
1 watt	10^7 ergs/second
1 watt	0.001341 horsepower

Bibliography

Chapter 1. Seams of the Earth

Cox, Allen, ed. *Plate Tectonics and Geomagnetic Reversals.* San Francisco: W. H. Freeman and Company, 1973.

Uyeda, Seiya. *The New View of the Earth.* San Francisco: W. H. Freeman and Company, 1978.

Wilson, Tuzo, ed. *Continents Adrift and Continents Aground.* Readings from Scientific American. San Francisco: W. H. Freeman and Company, 1963–1976.

Wyllie, Peter J. *The Way the Earth Works.* New York: John Wiley and Sons, 1976.

Chapter 2. Surtsey, Iceland

Thorarinsson, Sigurdur. "Surtsey: Island Born of Fire." *National Geographic Magazine,* May 1965, pp. 713–726.

Thorarinsson, Sigurdur. *Surtsey.* New York: Viking Press, 1967.

Chapter 3. Fire Under the Sea

Heezen, Bruce, and Charles Hollister. *The Face of the Deep.* New York: Oxford University Press, 1971.

Heezen, Bruce, Marie Tharp, and M. Ewing. *The Floors of the Oceans: I. The North Atlantic.* Geological Society of America, Special Paper 65, 1959.

Menard, H.W. *Marine Geology of the Pacific.* New York: McGraw-Hill, 1964.

Chapter 4. Krakatau, West of Java

Decker, Robert W., and Djajadi Hadikusumo. "Results of the 1960 expedition to Krakatau." *Journal of Geophysical Research* 66, 1961, pp. 3497–3511.

Furneaux, R. *Krakatoa*. New Jersey: Prentice-Hall, 1964.
Symons, C. J., ed. *The Eruption of Krakatoa*. Royal Society Report of the Krakatoa Committee. 1888.

Chapter 5. Ring of Fire

Dewey, John F., and John M. Bird. "Mountain Belts and the New Global Tectonics." *Journal of Geophysical Research* 75, No. 14, 1970, pp. 2625–2647.
Sugimura, A., and Seiya Uyeda. *Island Arcs: Japan and Its Environs*. Amsterdam: Elsevier, 1973.
Toksoz, M. Nafi. "The Subduction of the Lithosphere." *Scientific American*, November 1975, pp. 88–98.

Chapter 6. Kilauea, Hawaii

Eaton, J. P., and K. J. Murata. "How Volcanoes Grow." *Science* 132, October 1960, pp. 925–938.
Macdonald, Gordon A., and Agatin Abbott. *Volcanoes in the Sea*. Honolulu: University of Hawaii Press, 1970.
Macdonald, Gordon A., and Douglass Hubbard. *Volcanoes of the National Parks of Hawaii*. Hawaii: Hawaii Natural History Association, 1978.
Stearns, Harold T. *Geology of the State of Hawaii*. Palo Alto, CA: Pacific Books, 1965.

Chapter 7. Hot Spots

Burke, Kevin, and J. Tuzo Wilson. "Hot Spots on the Earth's Surface." *Scientific American*, August 1976, pp. 46–57.
Dalrymple, G. Brent, E.A. Silver, and E.D. Jackson. "Origin of the Hawaiian Islands." *American Scientist* 61, No. 3, 1973, pp. 294–308.
Morgan, W. J. "Deep Mantle Convection Plumes and Plate Motions." *American Association of Petroleum Geologists Bulletin* 56, No. 1, 1972, pp. 203–213.

Chapter 8. Lava, Ash and Bombs

Francis, Peter. *Volcanoes*. Middlesex, England: Penguin Books, 1976.
Macdonald, Gordon A. *Volcanoes*. New Jersey: Prentice-Hall, 1972.
Williams, Howel, and A.R. McBirney. *Volcanology*. San Francisco: Freeman, Cooper and Co., 1979.

Chapter 9. Cones and Craters

Bullard, Fred M. *Volcanoes of the Earth.* Austin: University of Texas Press, 1976.

Green, Jack, and Nicholas M. Short, eds. *Volcanic Landforms and Surface Features.* New York: Springer-Verlag, 1971.

Tazieff, Haroun. *The Orion Book of Volcanoes.* New York: Orion Press, 1961.

Chapter 10. Roots of Volcanoes

Elder, John. *The Bowels of the Earth.* Oxford: Oxford University Press, 1978.

Wyllie, Peter. "The Earth's Mantle." *Scientific American,* March 1975, pp. 50–57.

Chapter 11. Origin of the Sea and Air

Anderson, A.T. "Some Basaltic and Andesitic Gases." *Reviews of Geophysics and Space Physics* 13, 1975, pp. 37–55.

Holland, Heinrich D. *The Chemistry of the Atmosphere and Oceans.* New York: Wiley-Interscience, 1978.

Stoiber, R. E., and A. Jepsen. "Sulfur Dioxide Contributions to the Atmosphere by Volcanoes." *Science* 182, 1973, pp. 577–578.

Chapter 12. Volcanic Power

Barnea, Joseph. "Geothermal Power." *Scientific American,* January 1972, pp. 70–77.

Kruger, P., and C. Otte, eds. *Geothermal Energy.* Stanford, CA: Stanford University Press, 1973.

Muffler, L.J.P., ed. *Assessment of Geothermal Resources of the United States —1978.* U.S. Geological Survey Circular 790, 1979.

Chapter 13. Volcanic Treasures

Boyd, F. R., and Henry O.A. Meyer, eds. *Kimberlites, Diatremes, and Diamonds: Their Geology, Petrology, and Geochemistry.* Washington, D.C.: American Geophysical Union, 1979.

Park, Charles F., Jr., and Roy A. MacDiarmid. *Ore Deposits.* San Francisco: W.H. Freeman and Company, 1975.

Rona, Peter A. "Plate Tectonics and Mineral Resources." *Scientific American,* July 1973, pp. 86–95.

Chapter 14. Volcanoes and Climate

Lamb, H.H. *Climate: Present, Past, and Future*. London: Methuen, 1972.

Pollack, James B., Owen B. Toon, Carl Sagan, Audrey Summers, Betty Baldwin, and Warren Van Camp. "Volcanic Explosions and Climatic Change: A Theoretical Assessment." *Journal of Geophysical Research* 81, No. 6, 1976, pp. 1071–83.

Stommel, Henry, and Elizabeth Stommel. "The Year Without a Summer." *Scientific American*, June 1979, pp. 176–180.

Chapter 15. Forecasting Volcanic Eruptions

Crandell, Dwight R. and Donal R. Mullineaux. *Potential Hazards from Future Eruptions of Mount St. Helens Volcano, Washington*. U.S. Geological Survey Bulletin 1383-C. U.S. Government Printing Office, Washington, D.C., 1978.

Krüger, Christoph. *Volcanoes*. New York: G.P. Putnam's Sons, 1971.

Geophysics Study Committee, Geophysics Research Board, National Research Council. *Geophysical Predictions*. Washington D.C.: National Academy of Sciences, 1978.

Minakami, T., ed. *Surveillance and Prediction of Volcanic Activity*. Paris: UNESCO, Earth Science Monographs, 1972.

Appendix A. The World's 101 Most Notorious Volcanoes

International Association of Volcanology and Chemistry of the Earth's Interior. *Catalog of Active Volcanoes of the World, Parts I–XXII*. Rome, Italy, 1951–1975.

Smithsonian Institution. *Scientific Event Alert Network Bulletin*, Vol. 1–5. Washington, D.C., 1976–1980.

Volcanological Society of Japan. *Bulletin of Volcanic Eruptions*, Vol. 1–17. Tokyo, Japan, 1963–1979.

Index

Aa, 106–109
Airfall deposits, 103–104
Alvin, 35
Anak Krakatau, 43, 50, 51, 53–55
Anderson, Fred, 148
Andesite, 110, 113, 136
Andes Mountains, 9
Ash, volcanic, 20, 102–104
Atmosphere, origin of, 145–152
Azores, 30

Basalt, 75, 107, 110–115, 136
Bezymianny, 64, 67, 183, 206
Blocks, continental. See Continental crust
Bombs, volcanic, 19–20, 102–103

Calderas, 48–52, 126–128
    formation of, 48, 127
Cerro Negro, 57
Cinders, volcanic, 102, 108, 120
Climate, effects of volcanoes on, 44, 177–186
Complex volcanoes, 128
Composite volcanoes. See Strato-volcanoes
Compressional margins, 5, 8–9. See also Subduction zones
Cones, volcanic, 117–131
Contamination, 62
Continental drift, 2–4, 13
Cotopaxi, 117, 119

Crandell, Dwight, 203
Crater Lake, 127
Craters, 117–131
    formation of, 125–127
Crust, continental, 2, 8, 9, 13, 37, 60
    density of, 3
Crust, oceanic, 2, 8, 9, 13, 30, 37, 60
    density of, 3
Curtain of fire, 74, 78

Deformation monitoring, 194–196, 203
Density, 134–135
Diamonds, 135–136, 172–174
Dikes, volcanic, 120
Dormant volcano, 189

Earthquakes
    in eruption forecasting, 134, 189–193
    in Hawaii, 92–93, 191–192
    at plate boundaries, 8, 9, 191
Earthquake waves, 4, 10, 134
East Pacific ridge, 7, 8, 9
East Pacific rise. See East Pacific ridge
Eaton, Jerry, 70
Effusive eruptions, 69–84
Emperor Seamounts, 97–98
Explosive eruptions, 43–55, 63–64
Extensional margins, 5–10. See also Ridges, oceanic

Faults
  normal, 9
  thrust, 8
  transform, 9–10, 12. *See also*
    Strike-slip margin
Fire fountains, 70–78
Flank eruptions, 78, 80–84, 198–200
Forecasting eruptions, 187–208
Fracture zone, 10. *See also* Faults,
  transform; Strike-slip margin
Frictional heating, 61
Fyfe, William, 152

Galapagos Islands, 30, 98
Gases, volcanic, 32–35, 75, 145–152
  composition of, 148–149
  in eruption forecasting, 197–198
  origin of, 146–147
  volume of, 150–152
Geothermal power, 153–165
  at The Geysers, California, 160–161
  in Hawaii, 161–162
  in Iceland, 40, 41, 159–160
  at Larderello, Italy, 158–159
  See also Hot Dry Rock experiment;
    Magma energy research
Glowing avalanches. *See* Nuées
  ardentes
Graphite, 135–136, 172–173

Harmonic tremor. *See* Volcanic
  tremor
Hawaii, 29, 69–100, 129, 145
  map of, 72
Hawaiian chain, 88–91
  age map of, 91
Hawaiian-type eruptions, 69–87
Hawaiian Volcano Observatory,
  70–71, 73, 191, 198–200
Heat source, 137–139
Heat transfer, 157
Hekla, 16, 183, 189
Herdubreid, 125
Himalayas, 118
Hot Dry Rock experiment, 162–164
Hot-spot volcanoes, 87–99, 142

Iceland, 6, 5–27, 31, 37–40, 61, 99,
  119. *See also* Surtsey
Igneous rock types, 136
Indian Ocean ridge, 7–9

Island arcs, 58, 60–61, 141. *See also*
  Subduction zones

Japan, 9, 58, 60–61
Johnston, Dave, 206, 208

Kapoho eruption, 72, 78–86
Katmai, 64, 181, 183
Kennett, J.P., 182
Kilauea, 69–86, 109, 127–128,
  141–142, 190–196
Kilauea Iki, 69–85, 149, 164
Kimberley Diamond Pipe, 174
Krakatau, 43–55, 84, 179–181,
  183–184

Laki, 111, 120, 178–179
Lamb, H.H., 182
La Soufrière, Guadeloupe, 200
La Soufrière, St. Vincent, 181, 183,
  200, 202
Lava
  chemical composition of, 110,
    113–114
  temperatures of, 75, 78, 82,
    113–114
Lava dome, 120
Lava flow, 101, 106–111
Lava lake, 70, 75, 77–78, 87
Lava tubes, 110
Linear vents, 120
Los Alamos, 125–127
Los Alamos Scientific Laboratory,
  162–164
Low-velocity layer, 8–10, 13, 60,
  140–141

Magma, 32, 61, 92–96
  chemical composition of, 110,
    113–114
  deep source of, 92–93, 96
Magma chamber, 30, 48, 92–96,
  136–137
Magma energy research, 164
Magnetic field, 4–6
  in eruption forecasting, 196
Magnetic reversals, 5–6
Magnetic stripe pattern, 5–6, 96–97
Mantle, 8, 13, 60, 92, 96–97
Masaya, 124
Mauna Loa, 127–128, 198–200

Mayon, 119, 122
Mercury, 172
Microearthquakes, 71, 78, 94–95, 192
Mid-Atlantic ridge, 6–11, 16, 31, 35–37
Midway Island, 88
Mineral deposits, 61–62, 167–176
Mont Pelée, 64, 66, 104, 181, 183
Moore, Jim, 35, 148
Morgan, Jason, 97
Mother Lode, 169–170
Mount Agung, 183–185
Mount Fuji, 63, 119, 127
Mount Lassen, 123, 203
Mount Rainier, 131, 133
Mount St. Helens, 203–208
Mullineaux, Donal, 203

Neon, 147
Ngauruhoe, 130
Nuées ardentes, 52, 104–105. See also Pyroclastic flows

Obsidian, 113
Old Faithful, 165
Ol Doinyo Lengai, 175
Oshima, 104

Pahoehoe, 101, 108–110
Pangaea, 3–4
Partial crystallization, 62, 113–115
Partial melting, 13, 62
Pele's hair, 78
Pillow lavas, 27, 32–36, 121, 125
Piton de la Fournaise, 107
Plate tectonics, 5–14, 95–96
Plume, 95, 97
Pompeii, 64, 65, 105
Powell, John Wesley, 134
Pumice, 48–49, 74, 110
Pyroclastic flows, 103, 116, 125. See also Nuées ardentes
Pyroclastics, 102–106

Radioactive dating, 88–91
Radioactive heat, 137–138
Radiocarbon dating, 65
Rhyolite, 110, 113, 136
Richter, Don, 70
Ridges, oceanic, 4, 6–11, 13, 30–41
Rift valleys, 35–37

Rift volcanism, 30–41, 142
Rift zones, 78, 82, 198–199
Ring of Fire, 57–68
   map of, 59
Rio Grande rift, 144
Roots, volcanic, 133–144, 168
Ruapehu, 130

San Andreas fault, 10, 12
Seafloor spreading. See Plate tectonics
Seamounts, 97–98
Sedimentary mud, 35–36
Seismic waves. See Earthquake waves
Seismograph, 71, 84, 134, 191, 193
Seismology, 4, 10, 134
   in volcano forecasting, 191–193
Shield volcanoes, 120, 128
Ship Rock, 121
Silica, 61–62, 75, 110, 113, 136
Snake River Plain, 98
Solar radiation, 44, 181
Stoiber, Richard, 148
Stratospheric aerosol layer, 182–184
Strato-volcano, 120, 124
Strike-slip margin, 5, 10–12. See also Faults, transform
Stromboli, 64
Subduction zones, 8–9, 13, 57–68, 142. See also Compressional margins
Submarine volcanism, 15–27, 30–42, 120–121. See also Rift volcanism
Sulfur emission, 150–152
Surtsey, 15–27, 84, 183

Taal, 197
Table mountains, 121, 125
Thermal gradient, 139–140, 155
Thorarinsson, Sigurdur, 16
Thunnel, R.C., 182
Tidal friction, 137–139
Tidal waves, 46–49
Tiltmeter, 71, 75, 82, 85, 193–195
Tokarev, P.I., 200
Tolbachik, 118, 200, 201
Tongariro, 130
Trench, oceanic, 7–9
Tsunami. See Tidal wave
Tungsten, 172

Valle Grande, 126–127, 129
Vein. See Mineral deposits

Vestmann Islands, 18
Vesuvius, 64–65, 177
Volcanic complex. *See* Complex volcano
Volcanic front, 61
Volcanic landforms, 117–131, 137
Volcanic neck, 120, 121
Volcanic products, 64, 100–116
Volcanic tremor, 192–193

Wave-cut terrace, 19
Wegener, Alfred, 2–4, 10, 13
Wexler, Harry, 181–182
Wilson, Tuzo, 93, 95–97

Yellowstone Park, 98, 142–143, 165, 176